CREEPY
CAPITAL

CREEPY CAPITAL

Ghost Stories of Ottawa and the National Capital Region

MARK LESLIE

DUNDURN
TORONTO

Copy editor: Jennifer McKnight
Design: Jennifer Gallinger
Cover design: Laura Boyle
Cover image: 123RF.com / Songquan Deng
Printer: Webcom

Library and Archives Canada Cataloguing in Publication

Leslie, Mark, 1969-, author
        Creepy capital : ghost stories of Ottawa and the National Capital Region
/ Mark Leslie.

Includes bibliographical references.
Issued in print and electronic formats.
ISBN 978-1-4597-3345-9 (paperback).--ISBN 978-1-4597-3346-6 (pdf).--
ISBN 978-1-4597-3347-3 (epub)

        1. Ghosts--Ontario--Ottawa. 2. Ghosts--National Capital Region (Ont. and Québec). 3. Haunted places--Ontario--Ottawa. 4. Haunted places--National Capital Region (Ont. and Québec). I. Title.

BF1472.C3L467 2016   133.109713'84   C2016-900377-9
                                                         C2016-900378-7

1 2 3 4 5   20 19 18 17 16

We acknowledge the support of the Canada Council for the Arts and the Ontario Arts Council for our publishing program. We also acknowledge the financial support of the Government of Canada through the Canada Book Fund and Livres Canada Books, and the Government of Ontario through the Ontario Book Publishing Tax Credit and the Ontario Media Development Corporation.

Printed and bound in Canada.

VISIT US AT
Dundurn.com | @dundurnpress | Facebook.com/dundurnpress | Pinterest.com/dundurnpress

Dundurn
3 Church Street, Suite 500
Toronto, Ontario, Canada
M5E 1M2

To Steve Gaydos, a dear lifelong pal and
as close to my heart as a brother.

We haunted some great places together in Ottawa, didn't we, boobie?

Here's to another thirty plus years of a friendship
that transcends friendships.

As Mackenzie King wrote about his best friend in his 1906 book
The Secret of Heroism, you are "the man I loved as I have loved
no other man, my father and brother alone excepted."

Contents

"There is no proof of the existence of ghosts and spirits, but there is plenty of evidence for their presence. The evidence takes the form of ghost stories. On the basis of such evidence it is safe to conclude: Ghosts are good for us because they encourage us to face the greatest mysteries of all: life, death, fate, destiny, spirit, grace, damnation, salvation, deliverance, duty, and … above all … simple curiosity."

— John Robert Colombo, *Ghost Stories of Canada*

Foreword

I love ghost stories. And Ottawa, my hometown, is no stranger to the paranormal.

This first thing most people think of when they picture Canada's capital city is that it's home to the prime minister and many of our national institutions. Walk Ottawa's streets and you'll come across museums, galleries, the Royal Canadian Mint, the Department of National Defence, and, of course, the Parliament Buildings. Many of these imposing gothic buildings are older than Canada itself. As calm and peaceful as the city is today, it used to be a rough and lawless community. Following construction of the Rideau Canal many of the immigrant workers from England, Ireland, Scotland, and France formed gangs in an attempt to secure work. With little police presence, these gangs were largely left to their own devices and settled disputes without the authorities getting involved. As you can imagine, many of these disputes ended with the spilling of blood. So it should come as no surprise that, although Ottawa now enjoys a reputation as a safe and quiet city, there are many restless spirits haunting its streets.

The city, with its dark history hidden around every corner, is a major source of my fascination with ghosts. During the past few years I've spent a great deal of time researching and writing about the country's paranormal population for Scholastic Canada's bestselling Haunted Canada book series. I'm an advisor, writer, and researcher for Canada Post's new line of Haunted Canada stamps. On the day the first set of stamps were released

(Friday the 13th, naturally) I appeared on CTV's *Canada AM* to share the stamps' famous ghost stories, such as the ghost bride of the Banff Springs Hotel. And if that wasn't enough, I voluntarily checked into one of the most haunted hotels in the country, Niagara-on-the-Lake's Olde Angel Inn, and filmed myself through the night as I searched for spirits. Needless to say, I got very little sleep.

I have no doubt this paranormal preoccupation stems from my Ottawa upbringing and, even more specifically, a class trip to one of its most haunted locations, the Ottawa Jail Hostel, formerly the Carleton County Gaol.

With multiple reports of ghost sightings and a dark reputation as a site of sinister past deeds, the jail might seem like an odd location for a fifth-grade field trip. But that's the type of city Ottawa is — none of the adults who had a hand in the planning of the trip, from the teachers to the tour guide to the parents who happily signed the permission forms,

A 1971 statue of Lieutenant-Colonel John By (1779–1836), founder of Bytown, overlooks Parliament, the Rideau Canal, and the Bytown Museum from Major Hill's Park, behind the Château Laurier.

blinked an eye about sending a group of young and impressionable children to a building with an unmarked grave that's choked with bodies hidden beneath its parking lot.

You'll read more about the Ottawa Jail Hostel in this book, but if you ever have the opportunity to visit — or, better yet, spend a night in the hostel — don't hesitate. Stepping through the stone archway into the jail was something of a transcendent experience for me at the tender age of ten. The guide took a morbid pleasure in sharing tales of public executions, the horrible conditions in which the inmates lived, and the stairwell that is rumoured to have been the location of secret executions — unrecorded killings that created a surplus of bodies that needed to be hidden … so into the ground beneath the parking lot they went.

Those macabre stories weren't necessary to conjure up ghosts in my imagination — the building is creepy enough to do that on its own. And so is much of Ottawa. Take a trip with this book as your personal guide and you'll see what I mean.

By the time you return home, chances are you'll never view Ottawa in the same light again.

Joel A. Sutherland

Introduction

Ottawa is a very special place to me for numerous reasons.

As an attendee of Carleton University, Ottawa was my very first home away from home — the first city I moved to when I moved away from my parents' home at the age of nineteen.

But, most intriguingly, it was where I discovered the special magic that can happen when ghostly tales allow you to explore and better understand the history of a place.

I'll never forget the first ghost walk that I went on. It was the one that starts on the corner of Sparks Street and Elgin, just outside D'Arcy McGee's Irish Pub. It was a cool, late-summer evening, and there was a sense of excitement and nervous tension in the crowd of us who huddled in a group before the woman dressed in black, flowing Victorian-style robes and holding a lantern. Most of the folks gathered that evening had never been on a ghost walk before and did not know what to expect.

I expected to have chills run up and down my spine; that, of course, happened wonderfully throughout the evening. I expected to learn some fascinating and intriguing stories about ghosts in the area, unrolled in a creative and tantalizing story arc, and I most certainly did. But something else happened that I did not at all expect. Something that forever changed my perspective about the world.

I fell in love with history.

That might seem like a mundane thing to acknowledge, but it's pretty significant. You see, growing up, history was one of the subjects I most hated in school. Okay, I was never all that good at math, but at least I could find relevance in understanding and being able to solve particular problems. History had always seemed to be taught in such a boring and disconnected way to me. It was flat, and about boring people and boring times that seemed to have absolutely no relevance to me and my life. I suppose, given that I was a teenager during much of my first exposures to history, my mind wasn't all that open to the things being shared.

I felt that way until I was treated to the multiple history lessons brilliantly embedded within the creepy tales shared on the ghost walk of downtown Ottawa. That night, history came alive, and the tales of ghosts were made much more fascinating because of the manner by which they

The Rideau Canal lower locks, nestled between the Château Laurier and the Bytown Museum.

Author's collection.

drifted in, spectres born from the ripples of time, from all of the interesting things that had happened here in this city I so adore.

I didn't just learn about ghosts that night. I learned far more about the history of the city of Ottawa, of the Parliament Buildings and the Rideau Canal, not to mention details about the culture and politics of this fine city and our great nation.

Thus, when sharing ghostly tales, I've found it important to reach down into the depths of history and paint the scene with elements of that rich past dripping from the brush. Understanding the times, the people, and the places as they were in the past brings a richer sense of appreciation in our present.

I have tried to do the same thing in this book, as well as my other explorations of the paranormal. In *Haunted Hamilton* I explored a great deal about the people and times, in particular the effect that the War of 1812 had on the city and the many ghostly tales that resulted. *Spooky Sudbury* reached all the way back to the formation of the Sudbury Basin and the rich nickel deposits that resulted from a meteorite crash in prehistoric times. And in *Tomes of Terror* there was a respect paid to the magic that happens in libraries and bookstores, places that are dedicated to books — that incredible creation that so eloquently captures all that humanity itself has to offer.

Researching and writing this book has rekindled my love and passion for a city that I spent many formative years in, and that will always hold a special place in my heart. But it has also been very much a homecoming, a return to that very first realization that ghost stories and historic tales can merge in a spectacular *danse macabre*.

In the spring of 2015, I returned to Ottawa with my intrepid research assistant Liz to finalize research for this book, and to again explore the city via the wonderful Haunted Walk tours. The magic, the wonder, and the sense of eeriness filled our minds and hearts as we trekked through the cold Ottawa night and listened to fascinating tales about Ottawa's dark history and the ghosts that creep stealthily through the city's streets.

Now it is time for you and I to walk those dark streets together, take a peek into the history, the violence, and danger inherent in this locale once known as Bytown, into the city where people who formed our great nation resided, and where those who should have passed on to other worlds continue to reside, skulking through the shadows, whispering to us from the past, and reminding us that there are, indeed, more things in heaven and earth than are dreamt of in our philosophies.

Come, take my hand.

Let's explore the dark corners, the deep rich shadows of the past, the tales best told in the dark thick of the night.

Let's walk together and I shall share with you a few fascinating things I have learned about the city of Ottawa and the surrounding region.

Acknowledgements

As always, when it comes to thanking everybody who helped me with a book, there are always so many people along the way who I'm more likely to accidentally leave out than remember to include. My biggest fear at this point is doing just that. Because regardless of how minor it might have felt to the person who was assisting me, it is always so greatly appreciated, likely far more than the person lending the hand might ever know.

I would first like to thank folks from the following locations: the Bytown Museum, especially Sandy Trueman and Grant Vogl; staff from the Fairmont Château Laurier; and staff and guides from the HI-Ottawa Jail Hostel.

I owe a great deal of thanks to all of the wonderful people at Haunted Walks Inc. in Ottawa, especially Jim Dean, creative director, for providing photos of the amazing walks that inspired me to research, write, and share historical ghost stories, and to Glen Shackleton, founder, not just for the walks but the books he has written.

Matthew Didier, founder and director of the Ontario Ghosts and Hauntings Research Society, was also very gracious with his time, resources, and permissions, and I am truly grateful for his assistance and support.

Thanks to Joel A. Sutherland for writing the foreword for this book. Joel is not only a talented writer and a wonderful person (not to mention a librarian, one of my favourite types of people — but then again, aren't all book people amazing?), but he's also proof that writers look out for and are supportive of one another. You'd be doing yourself a favour to check out his books. In a similar fashion, I owe thanks to John Robert Colombo, who not only also wrote a foreword for my previous book, but also mentored me in the collecting of haunted stories, provided advice and encouragement along the way, and inspired me with his own writing. Dundurn has published a good number of John's books, several of which are referenced in this book, and they are also worth seeking out.

As always, the team at Dundurn is amazing to work with. Thank you to Beth, Karen, James, Margaret, Jaclyn, and Sheila for all of the ongoing support throughout the year. And a huge shout out to Kathryn Lane and Jennifer McKnight for their editorial insights and helping me take a decent submitted manuscript and crafting it into something I can be truly proud of.

And finally, a special thank you to Liz Anderson, my partner, not just in this life journey, but in the many fun adventures we share along the way. Her assistance, encouragement, support, and inspiration throughout the process of putting this book together are appreciated more than I could ever express. I especially want to thank her for holding my hand, having my back, and ensuring that none of the ghosts got me while we were researching some of the haunted locales.

Map of Downtown Ottawa

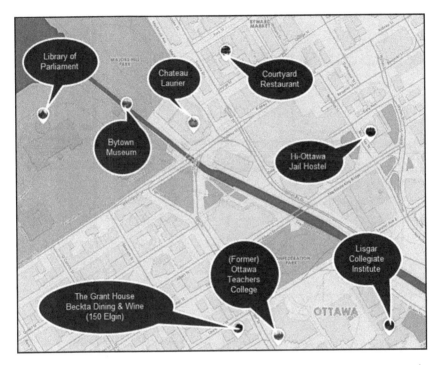

A map of downtown Ottawa, showing eight of the locations mentioned in this book. A full map of many of the *Creepy Capital* locales can be found on Mark Leslie's Pinterest page at www.pinterest.com/markleslie/creepy-capital.

The Grant House
at 150 Elgin

On a chilly Halloween eve in 2014, just days prior to the grand re-opening of Beckta Dining & Wine, owner Stephen Beckta drank champagne from a 140-year-old glass that once belonged to the Grant family, who used to live at that residence.

When questioned as to whether the stories he had heard about the building's history and the alleged spirit still there concerned him, Beckta shrugged and said with a laugh, "Not at all."

But not everybody else is so brave in their approach.

The building at 150 Elgin Street was originally built for Doctor James Alexander Grant in 1875. Designed by Bradish Billings Jr., the home, considered a mansion, cost approximately $11,000 to build at a time when the average home's cost was less than half of that.

Born on August 11, 1831, in Inverness, Scotland, James Grant came to Canada as an infant. His parents settled in Glengarry, Ontario, about an hour's drive southeast of Ottawa. There, Grant's father set up a medical practice and established himself as a one of the region's most distinguished physicians. Grant followed in his father's footsteps by receiving his undergraduate degree at the University of Queen's College (Queen's University) in Kingston, then moved on to study medicine at McGill College in Montreal. He became a medical doctor in 1854 and established a practice in Ottawa. Grant married Maria Malloch in 1856 and the two had a dozen children together.

Further following in his father's footsteps, Dr. James Alexander Grant ran a very successful medical practice. Due to his renowned skills and relentless work ethic he became known and sought out by many of the more prominent members of the local community.

Grant published several articles in medical journals in Canada and England and his vast interest and knowledge in the scientific fields led to his role as a charter member of the Royal Society of Canada. In addition, he served as president of the College of Surgeons on Ontario and the Mechanics' Institute and Athenaeum of Ottawa. Grant also served as the official physician for the Governors General from 1867 to 1905.

Grant also became involved in politics. He served as a member of Parliament for the Conservative Party between 1867 and 1874, as well as between 1893 and 1896.

After he saved the life of Queen Victoria's daughter, Princess Louise, when she had a sleigh accident near Rideau Hall, Grant was knighted Sir James Grant and he was awarded the Most Distinguished Order of St Michael and King George (KCMG).

Grant died on June 5, 1920, after having lived at his Elgin Street home for nearly half a century.

Given the status that he held and his long-time association with the building, it's no wonder that when tales of odd and eerie occurrences started being reported people's thoughts turned to Sir James Alexander Grant. Perhaps Grant's role as a physician — which included stories that the basement of the residence at 150 Elgin was used as a morgue — has been a factor in some of the ghostly tales that are shared about the building.

After the Grant family moved out of the home, the building was purchased by the University of Ottawa's University Club. In the late sixties and early seventies, highway-construction projects threatened the building and in 1974 the city came under attack for what was described as its "lack of interest in preserving a historic property." A proposal was made to bring a sixty-bed youth hostel to the building, but it never came to fruition. What finally took over the building was a restaurant known as Friday's Roast Beef House, which occupied the site from 1972 to 2009.

During that era was when most of the tales alluding to a ghost within the building's walls started to come out.

The majority of sightings and ghostly encounters have taken place in the second- and third-floor hallways. Well after the building had been closed and almost empty, restaurant staff reported hearing the distinct sound of footsteps descending the stair, only to witness that stairway completely empty.

Both patrons and staff have shared stories of being shoved or pushed by unseen hands, and some have reportedly fallen sideways over the banister. In each case, the person who fell claimed the sensation of unseen hands pushing them. Members of the Haunted Walk of Ottawa shared that a woman who had been on one of their tours claimed that exact thing happened to her before the tour guide had a chance to share any stories about the building. The unseen presence responsible for these actions has also knocked trays mysteriously out of the staff's hands.

Courtesy of Haunted Walks Inc.

Three Haunted Walk tour guides on Elgin Street, uphill from where they share tales of the Grant House.

Restaurant staff have also reported several occasions when, after they had closed for the night, they heard the sound of laughter echoing in from the empty piano bar, or their name being called out when there was nobody else around.

There was one particular table on the second floor that seemed prone to icy cold breezes, and objects on the table were reported to have moved entirely of their own volition. Cliff Scott, the author of *Ottawa Stories: Trials & Triumphs in Bytown History*, mustered the courage to sit there with his wife for dinner one evening. Scott reported feeling nothing other than a little bit of trepidation, as well as the eyes of the other patrons, who were likely all there waiting to witness something supernatural.

The second floor seems to be at the centre of the ghostly tales. And whispers are still shared about the spectral image of an elderly man seen sitting at a second-floor window well after the restaurant was closed and all staff had gone home.

Among the most eerie of incidents to have been reported at 150 Elgin when it was Friday's Roast Beef House are the stories of staff and guests, who described hearing the odd sound of some unseen person breathing heavily right next to them. The combination of wheezing and hacking cough is a consistent description, which ties in quite interestingly to the fact that Sir James Alexander Grant had been a sufferer of severe asthma for most of his life.

Stephen Beckta, the aforementioned restaurateur and owner of Beckta Dining & Wine, has begun the latest chapter of this historic building on the solid footing of creating something new and unique while taking great care to both respect and preserve history. "This is a legacy project that will outlive us by far," Beckta said in an interview with the *Ottawa Citizen*.

Beckta and Peter Weiss, project manager for PCL Construction Company, put together a time capsule, which includes a history of the legacy building, an outline of the design of the twenty-three-storey tower that now adjoins the building, an historic letter from 1932 that was found in the home, and one of the crested Grant-family glasses that Beckta drank champagne out of while celebrating the pre-opening of his gorgeous new restaurant. The capsule is sealed in a back wall of the building with a glass plaque, visible from the Winter Garden atrium that connects the historic building to the newly constructed tower. Etched on the glass is a line from the late Bob Marley: "In this great future you can't forget your past."

"I told Dr. Grant that we were going to take good care of his house," Stephen Beckta said in an interview with Danika Grenier, digital content manager of Ottawa Tourism. "And ever since then, everything seems to have been going swimmingly. So if there is a ghost, he likes us in this space."

The Normal School Ghost

One security guard working in a city hall building on Elgin and Lisgar was not able to return to work due to the debilitating nightmares he experienced and another security guard refused to work the night shift after each experienced a terrifying run-in with the building's ghost.

And the ghost, who seems to think the building is still a school, rather than the location that houses Ottawa's mayor, appears to be there to teach a thing or two to the local municipal leaders.

The Gothic Revival Heritage Building at 195 Elgin, which is now a part of Ottawa City Hall, was originally built in 1875 as Ottawa Normal School, part of Ontario's normal school system of teacher's colleges that had been set up by Egerton Ryerson (the same Ryerson that the Toronto University is named after).

In 1953 the school was renamed the Ottawa Teacher's College. In 1974, after it was decided that Ontario's teacher's colleges would merge into the university systems, the college joined the Faculty of Education at the University of Ottawa, and the building was sold to the federal government in 1978.

The Regional Municipality of Ottawa-Carleton purchased the building in 1986, and it was renamed the Heritage Building, which houses the mayor's office.

When the building was a teacher's college, the front section of the building was where the teachers went to class and took courses, but

James William Topley, 1893.

Ottawa Normal School was designed by architect W.R. Strickland and built by J. Forin. Designated as a national historic site in 1974, the building is recognized as a significant example of Gothic revival architecture in Canada.

farther back down a long hallway was a "model school" where the student teachers taught real students in an actual classroom setting.

One of the earliest instructors at the school was a woman by the name of Eliza Bolton, who taught some of the very first kindergarten teachers from the 1880s. Bolton retired in 1917, but not before she was responsible for making a change to the school policy that required a single teacher to have to supervise two classrooms. This new rule meant that teachers would have to constantly move back and forth between two different classrooms.

Some believe that Bolton's change to the system might be what prompts her ghost to continue to move quickly about the building, between various rooms, opening and closing doors.

In 1998 a security guard working the night shift alone in the Heritage Building spotted her down the end of a hallway that runs the length of the old model school. Wearing old-fashioned clothing, the woman was coming out of one of the classrooms and headed for the classroom directly across the hall. The guard called out to her, asking her who she was, and she stopped, turned toward him, and looked him straight in the eye. Then she quickly turned around and headed back into the room she had just left.

The guard ran after her, but when he entered the room he found it completely empty — the mysterious woman had disappeared. There were no other exits from the classroom other than the doorway he had just passed through. He left the classroom confused and wondering if he had been seeing things.

Then, later on during his shift, when he passed a display case in the lobby, he spied a photograph from the old teacher's college and recognized the face and style of the woman he had seen disappear into the classroom earlier that evening.

This guard refused to ever work the night shift alone again.

In the past several years, security guards have had so many encounters with a ghost that they believe to be the spirit of Eliza Bolton that they have started to tease and play practical jokes on one another. They have been known to hide their walkie-talkies in various spots in the building, setting them off in order to scare rookie guards, and also to place a life-sized cut-out of a woman dressed in old fashioned clothing in various dark corners and doorways in order to surprise or startle one another.

But not every startling incident is caused by fellow employees.

On a particularly hot evening in July of 2001, a guard nearing the end of his shift was walking through his final rounds and headed up to walk through the attic. When he arrived at the attic he immediately felt that something was wrong. During the hot summer months the attic was normally stiflingly hot, and on a night such as that one it should have been almost unbearably stuffy and hot. But he found the attic was extremely cold — startlingly cold. As he walked through a fog began to appear, and in it was the glowing figure of a woman wearing old-fashioned clothing.

"Get back to class," she said to him in a soft yet stern voice.

The guard ran as fast as he could out of the attic, but he didn't stop to enter a classroom, as she had suggested. Instead, he ran straight out the first set of doors he came to, eager to put as much distance as he could between himself and the terrifying apparition he had seen.

The guard eventually quit his job, sharing that he had continued to have terrifying nightmares about the experience.

Although there are plenty more recent ghostly tales involving this building and encounters with the ghost of Eliza Bolton, there are some that aren't all that new, having been shared for generations.

During my research I found a story published in the *1916–17 Year Book of the Ottawa Normal School*. While I'm not sure if the story is meant to be fiction or a documented true tale, it is certainly intriguing to read the words of students and their perspective on just what this ghost could be. Of course, in their case, the ghost isn't that of a teacher but that of a student.

The Ghost of the Normal School
By R. Pearl Chamney and Myrtle H. Adams

I had often heard of the Ghost that haunts the Normal School, but being somewhat of a sceptic, doubted its existence. Several students have declared that a shadowy apparition has been seen by some of their number, flitting in at the door at the back of the gallery room, gliding down the steps, and disappearing in a mysterious manner. Now, the time was when I myself would have laughed at these affirmations and I would in my innermost thoughts have considered the propounder of such as fit to rank with the common multitude and as having no place whatever in the cultured halls of the Normal School. But even we who pride ourselves on being proof against all superstition are likely to have our firmest ideas uprooted, and thereby to become susceptible to ghostly visions.

I was busily engaged one evening after school in the laboratory on the "Verification of the Law of Inverse

Squares." Absorbed in my work I became utterly oblivious of the passing of time. When I had worked for what seemed to me a very short time I glanced casually at my watch and was startled to find by the pale glimmer of the candle which I was using that it was already past eight o'clock. A feeling of dread crept over me at the thought of being alone in this great building.

Although I tried to assure myself that I was not in the least frightened my heart beat a little more rapidly as I crept stealthily toward the door of the laboratory. Suddenly a cold chill spread over me and I began to shiver. This indescribable feeling grew so intense that when I reached the door my teeth were chattering, my knees were shaking (as no Normal students ever did when called upon to teach), and my fingers were so numb that I had difficulty in forcing the doorknob to yield to their grasp.

The story of the Ghost of the Normal flashed before my mind in its most dreadful aspects, but knowing that fear is an emotion unworthy of any Normal student, I attempted to drive it from me and vainly endeavoured to recall the "Three Level Theory" instead. I finally pulled the door open, and, horror of horrors! what a ghastly apparition stood facing me! My hair stood on end, my flesh began to creep, my knees knocked together and my teeth chattered. I realized now that the legend of the Normal ghost was only too true. The Awful Thing stood in the pale yellow glimmer of the moonlight that struggled in through the partly shaded window of the little laboratory. It glared at me from the depths of its greenish eyes. It clasped in its claw-like fingers a number of books, which I recognized as similar to those used in our class-rooms.

"Who are you?" I asked, with all the decision I could muster.

"I am the ghost of one long gone before," was the reply in sepulchral tones. "Once I was a happy Normal student like you, but ambition sealed my fate. I hoped to write text-books on Psychology, History of Education, Geography, Science, Music, Art, Hygiene and Grammar, and incidentally to discover scientific truths, write stories and travel in foreign lands, but, alas! my brain refused to sustain the pressure. I come nightly to haunt these rooms and continue my scientific researches. Take warning, fair student, Ambition's debt is dearly paid."

I was glad that I had not attempted to combat my ghostly visitor, for I am told that physical forces do not avail in the presence of such supernatural beings, but that it is more effective to appeal to their intellect.

Before the Awful Thing had ceased my temperature had dropped considerably from ninety-eight and three-fifths degrees. Such an unnatural condition caused my whole body to tremble. I was about to fall prostrate, when lo! the horrible apparition began slowly, slowly to fade away. Under the hypnotic spell of the late spectre my eyes remained glued to the spot where it had stood, but in the pale moon-light all that I saw was that gruesome skeleton which we use in our hygiene class.

Solving the Mystery of That Dog-Gone Ghost

Following is an article from the August 6, 1932, issue of the *Ottawa Citizen*. It recounts a slightly humorous story of how an incident at an old log house in Nepean, long believed to be haunted, sent the males in a family into quite the tizzy before they learned the truth about what had been causing the ghostly ruckus.

The Family Dog Ended Ghost Story
Mr. Robert Cummings of Nepean Tells Tale of How Family Dog and a Strap of Sleigh Bells Caused Excitement In An Old House Which Had Reputation of Being Haunted

Mr. Robert Cummings, son of the late James Cummings of the 3rd line (R.F.) of Nepean, tells a ghost story with a humorous ending. Mr. Cummings lives on the old Kelly farm. The incident happened when he was a small boy about 40 years ago. On the Kelly farm, when the Cummings family went there first there was an old log house which had the reputation of being haunted. The Cummings used the old place as a storehouse. Among other things, they kept oats there. One night after dark

John W. Cummings, a brother of Robert, had to go to the old place to get some oats. As he opened the door he heard bells ringing and feet descending the stairs. 'Twas enough. He closed the door and ran home. He called his brother, W.J., his brother Bob and his father, and told them the place was really haunted. They went with him. Sure enough, when Pa Cummings opened the door, he also heard the bells and then heard feet descending the stairs. He closed the door.

Held Conference

Then the four held a conference to decide on a line of action. Pa's advice was to throw the door wide open and await further developments.

"Whatever it is in there will likely come out," he said. They threw the door open and waited, each armed with a stout stick.

They had not long to wait. Out came the family dog, wagging its tail. The animal had got shut in earlier in the evening. Nothing more ghostly came.

The Explanation

The next morning, Mr. Cummings went to the old place to try and find an explanation of the bells that had been heard. He found one. It appears that in the loft there had hung from a peg on the wall a string of sleigh bells. Underneath the bells had been an old rug on which the dog had made itself comfortable. Whenever the dog got up its back struck the string of bells, causing it to ring. When the dog heard the door open it trotted downstairs.

Other Stories Told

Mr. Robert Cummings says that despite easy explanation of the dog and the bells, the old house had many other queer stories told of it by neighbors who declared they had heard and seen things in and around the place.

A few years after the incident referred to, Mr. Cummings Sr. had had the place pulled down. With the destruction of the building its ghostly reputation had ceased.

The Conversion of Skeptics at the Bytown Museum

Two types of skeptics are regularly converted after spending some time in the Bytown Museum: those who believe that Ottawa has always been a quiet, mundane, and somewhat sleepy capital, and those who believe that ghosts are merely the figment of an overly hyper imagination.

From the Iroquois, Algonquin, and Huron people who settled in the area dating back as far as 8000 BCE, through the French explorers and Jesuit missionaries of the 1700s to the Great Fires of 1870 and 1900, there was rarely a time when the region could ever properly be considered quiet or sleepy. On a self-guided tour of the Bytown Museum (1 Canal Lane; www.bytownmuseum.com), armed with a headset and audio player, patrons move through a series of numbered locations and are treated to a uniquely wonderful immersion in the various stages of the city's and the country's growth. Presented with artifacts, sounds, videos, and authentic descriptions it would be hard for anybody to leave the Bytown Museum without a deeper respect and understanding of the various intriguing trials, tragedies, and triumphs that echo through the ages.

And in the same way that the museum helps history come alive, so too does it often cause visitors to speculate in the manner that Hamlet did of there being "more things in heaven and earth … than are dreamt

The Bytown Museum, seen in the background, helps history come alive for visitors.

Author's collection.

of" in our philosophies. Many believe that the building is haunted by a man from the very earliest days of the building's long history.

Dating back to 1827 and being marked as the oldest stone building in Ottawa, the Bytown Museum was originally Lieutenant-Colonel John By's commissariat. A commissariat is a type of warehouse where military supplies and funding for workers and contractors are stored. And, being a place where items of great importance and value were kept, it was believed to be an easy target for theft.

The building was guarded by a supply manager named Duncan Macnab. Macnab, whose job was to protect the gold and silver, the military arms and supplies, and the thick rock walls, must have been quite effective because there is no indication or record of there ever being any theft from the treasury or stores of the building while he was in charge.

Some believe that Macnab, so obsessed with the protection of the building, still lingers there long after his death, ensuring that his vigilant presence is felt.

Some speculate that the haunting is due to the thousands of workers who died in the construction of the nearby Rideau Canal, due to accidents and the spread of diseases such as malaria.

Still others believe that Lieutenant-Colonel John By, the founder of Bytown, who died in 1836, still wanders along the canal that he oversaw the completion of between 1826 and 1832, and is an additional presence in the building.

About one third of the way through the self-guided tour of the museum, visitors are instructed by the audio's narrative to peer out the second-floor windows to see, directly across the canal, at the edge of Major's Hill Park, a statue with the likeness of Lieutenant-Colonel By. I couldn't help but be overcome with an odd feeling of being watched, perhaps even scrutinized. *Was it just the statue of Colonel John By?* I wondered, suspecting the phenomenon came from within my own perception. *Or is there something else ... someone else, someone inside watching me?*

I had, after all, heard the story of how two museum employees were discussing the possibility of the building being haunted by By when the computer in front of them turned itself off all on its own. When it booted back up, again on its own, the only thing that appeared on the monitor over and over were the words:

Lt. Col. John By

Lt. Col. John By

Lt. Col. John By

Lt. Col. John By

It was almost as if the colonel had been listening to the conversation and wanted to make it perfectly clear that he was still around, still watching and listening.

That might have been the way Glen Shackleton, director and founder of Haunted Walks Inc., initially felt when experienced something odd at what has been described as one of Ottawa's most haunted locations.

Shackleton, who heads up the historic ghost walks of downtown Ottawa, has also spent a significant amount of time in the Bytown

Museum acting as one of the building's volunteers. Having heard plenty of ghost stories associated with several different locations from many different people, Shackleton was aware of the possibility that a spooky historic location combined with an overactive imagination might very well be the real cause of the stories he had heard about the museum. But a series of incidents that happened to him in that very building changed his mind.

One of the stories that has been repeatedly shared about the museum involves the stairs. Visitors regularly indicate that they heard the sound of heavy footsteps on the stairs behind them, but when they stopped and turned there was nobody there. Despite this fact, they would claim to hear the footsteps continue on past them.

Shackleton's original belief was that the old wood of the stairs could possibly be making the noise, due to them being compressed by the visitor's own upward steps and then slowly released back a second after they moved on, creating the eerie footstep-like sound.

But one afternoon in 2006 he was in the middle of a conversation with the museum's program coordinator, Steve, while the two of them were walking together. When Shackleton headed up the stairs, he kept talking, positive that the other man was following directly behind him. When Shackleton turned to ask a question, he realized that Steve was no longer there. He had forgotten something and turned around, remaining behind on the main floor. But despite being alone on the stairs, Shackleton not only heard the distinct sound of footsteps but also felt a distinct presence lurking around him.

After previously being skeptical about the reports he had heard, Shackleton stopped discounting the phenomenon of the sound of footsteps on the stairs.

Other phenomena shared about the building include motion detectors going off in the middle of the night when the building is securely locked and empty. The historical videos, which are typically triggered by somebody pressing a nearby button, have also turned on and off all by themselves.

One employee at the museum believed that the ghost was a mischievous fellow, and found the incidents more annoying than frightening.

One afternoon she was working in an adjacent room and the audio of Wade Hemsworth's classic folk song "The Log Drivers' Waltz" kept turning on by itself.

As the chorus of the song blasted out yet again, this particular employee was not at all pleased. She was so frustrated, in fact, that she yelled out, "Stop that! You know I hate that song!"

Immediately following her outburst, the music stopped.

Some believe, based on incidents like this one, that at least one of the ghosts that calls the museum home is a bit of a playful spirit. Duncan Macnab, the aforementioned guard and storekeeper of the commissariat, also had a bit of a reputation as a trickster. When some rum went missing, Macnab explained the disappearance as it having "evaporated," despite the incident taking place in the dead of winter. And a man who had died continued to receive his full rations for a week after his death, at least, according to the records. It seems as if Duncan Macnab, who enjoyed playing tricks on people back in the 1820s, might very well still be responsible for some of the odd and playful incidents taking place in the building today, including moving pieces of furniture around, the lights and videos turning on and off, as well as a distinct disembodied male voice shouting "get out."

Part of an exhibit of what it was like for a child growing up in Ottawa nearly two hundred years ago included a row of children's dolls. Macnab might very well have been the one who took possession of the dolls that used to be part of that exhibit, although many think that they were being animated by the spirit of a dead child. When I arrived at the museum in the winter of 2015, eager to see the dolls I had heard and read so much about, I was disappointed to learn that they had since been removed. Perhaps that's a good thing, because even the thought of catching one of these cute inanimate childhood playthings winking at me, or hearing soft child-like crying coming from the area where the dolls were located sets the hair on the back of my neck on end and throws a cold shiver down my spine.

The schoolhouse artifacts that were there — a desk, slate tablets, and abacus, the mirrors featuring headless children wearing period clothing (meant to make the child standing in front of the mirror see what they

might look wearing those clothes), along with the black shoeprints leading deeper into the display — were quite enough to kick my imagination
into high gear.

To close this chapter, let's have a look at a situation that Glen Shackleton
describes as "certainly one of the most frightening moments" of his life.

At the end of a nighttime staff meeting with his haunted-walk group
at the Irish pub D'Arcy McGee's, Shackleton realized that he had forgotten to set the alarm at the museum, which was a couple of blocks away.
Two of the tour guides from his company, Margo and Emily, as well as
Emily's mother, joined him as he set forth in the dark, down the hill
toward the museum.

Because they were accompanied by the mother of one of the guides,
Shackleton decided to show her some of the more interesting artifacts in
the museum, including the death hand of D'Arcy McGee. In the Victorian
era, it was common to make plaster casts of the faces of famous people
after they had died. But because McGee had been shot in the head (making it impossible for a proper face cast to be made), a cast was created of
his hand.

The cast is in a display on the third floor of the museum, so all four of
them ascended so that Emily and her mother could check out the display.
At that point, Shackleton and Margo wandered back down to the second
floor. That was when they both heard footsteps coming up the stairs from
the first to the second floor. The sound was so loud and so distinct that
Shackleton and Margo shared an "are you hearing what I'm hearing?" look
before peering around the corner. Despite the continuing sound of footsteps, there was nobody visible coming up the stairs.

Shackleton, always looking for a natural explanation for eerie phenomenon, wondered if the noise might be the echoes of the movement
of Emily and her mother on the floor above. But when he and Margo
rushed upstairs to check, they saw the two women standing still at the
very back of the room, reading the plaque that details D'Arcy McGee's
assassination and the trial of Patrick Whelan, the man charged with
his murder.

Author's collection.

The cast of Thomas D'Arcy McGee's hand. McGee, a politician and Father of Confederation, was assassinated by the Fenians.

The four then headed back down to the gift shop on the main floor, and Shackleton began the process of securing and locking the building while his companions waited near the main entrance.

As Shackleton was closing the wooden sliding door that had separated the gift shop from the rest of the building, he jokingly pointed out the security display and said in a loud voice that if anyone dared appear on camera in the room on the other side of that door, he would definitely be out of there in a hurry.

That's when an odd shaking sensation began. The sliding door started to swing and to shake; first quite slowly, but then, as the seconds passed, more vigorously. It appeared to Shackleton as if somebody on the other side of the door was violently tearing at it in an attempt to get out. Simultaneously, the souvenirs in the nearby gift shop began to shake and rattle.

Frozen in shock and in fear, Shackleton stood looking at the trembling door just inches from his face before turning to his friends to ask if they could see what was happening.

That's when he spotted them running quickly out the front door.

Margo, however, paused and ducked back into the gift shop. Shackleton abandoned his stance by the sliding door and joined her outside. The four of them stood in the cold night air, shaking their heads, trying to catch their breath, and sharing what they had each seen.

While Shackleton had experienced something pulling at the door, the other three had heard the sound of heavy footsteps walking across the ceiling above them.

All evidence suggested that at least one person, perhaps two, were still inside.

Shackleton finally managed the courage to go back inside, set the alarm, and lock the door.

The group stood outside the building for half an hour, convinced that they had just locked a pair of unseen intruders inside and that the motion detectors and alarms would soon be activated. Once they went off, they planned to phone the police, believing they would teach a lesson to whomever was inside, playing an eerie prank on them. But the motion detectors never went off, and the four finally went home for the night.

Shackleton still talks about how, when he arrived home that night and crawled into bed, he left the bedside light on the whole night.

Bytown's Haunted House

There have been a number of haunted houses dating back to Ottawa's early years, when it was known as Bytown. One of the more famous haunted houses from that era was a stately stone home that used to be on the south side of Wellington Street, near Bay.

The building was the home of Dr. Edward Van Cortlandt, a notable and prominent figure known as arguably the best physician in the Bytown area, but also for odd eccentrics, such as keeping a skeleton in his closet that he amused himself with by frightening patients. After the doctor died his house remained vacant, perhaps because of its reputation for being haunted.

Following is the full article from the *Ottawa Citizen* on April 29, 1933.

> **Ottawa As It Was In The Year 1893 —**
> **Wellington St. In "The Gay Nineties"**
> **Old Dr. Van Cortlandt House And Its Ghostly Stories**
> *House was Noted in Many Ways And Its Owner Was Remarkable Man — House, Long a Landmark, Has Been Removed. Van Courtlandt Home Was Outstanding Feature on Wellington Street.*
>
> In our walk down Wellington street last week we stopped at the southeast corner of Bay street where Philemon

Courtesy of Haunted Walks Inc.

A Haunted Walk guide leads a crowd down Sparks Street on a spooky journey through history, sharing eerie tales of the past.

Wright, the harness maker, a Bytonian, lived and had his place of business.

Today we start at the southwest corner where we encounter a pretty two-door stone tenement, fronted by attractive verandahs. These houses were built either in the late forties or early fifties. The present occupants (1893) are W. J. Loucks and John B. Gillesie.

Next (at 394) we come to a large three story and attic stone house which at the present time is occupied by Mrs. I. Aylen's boarding house. This is the famous old Van Cortlandt house, erected by the late Dr. Edward Van Cortlandt in the early fifties.

Dr. Van Cortlandt was noted as a surgeon but he had a large family practice. He had a great reputation as a geologist and naturalist, and delved into the Indian history of the Ottawa Valley. He was one of the most popular of the lecturers at the Mechanics Institute.

The Skeleton

The doctor was regarded as a bit eccentric, but his cleverness as a medical man, or his value as a citizen was never in question. In a deep cupboard in his office the doctor kept a skeleton dangling. It was so hung that whenever he opened the cupboard to get anything the bones rattled in a manner to frighten nervous people and children. Many old timers will relate how as children they were frightened by the Van Cortlandt skeleton. When the door was open the skeleton was never fully visible, and the fact created a story of mystery which made the skeleton all the more intriguing.

Very Thick Walls

The Van Cortlandt house had very thick walls. The window sills were fully three feet deep. The ceilings of the big house were high and the rooms large.

The house was built on the slant of the high hill which ran upward to Sparks street on a seven or eight per cent grade. This meant that the doctor could have his office on the level of Wellington street, while the kitchen and other culinary rooms were in the rear partly underground.

Access To Garden

The main or parlor floor was approached by steep steps from Wellington street. A narrow covered verandah fronted the house. The rear of the parlor and dining room led out on a level to a pretty garden, from which an exit could be had onto Sparks street.

The house had a large attic which was used for servants' quarters. In later years the attic played a considerable part in the ghost stories with which the old house became surrounded. In effect the house was four storeys high including the attic. From the Wellington street front it had an imposing appearance.

House Is Gone

The O.T.S. mentions these facts as the house is no longer in existence. A couple of years ago it was pulled down to make room for a mercantile building. Many Ottawa people were very sorry to see the old house go as it was a landmark.

Dr. "Van" as he was familiarly called, died about the year 1872 or 1873. After his death the house became vacant.

Stories Started

The doctor had not been long dead before stories spread that the house had become haunted. It is easy for such stories to come into existence. It's easier for them to spread. And they certainly spread in this case. Stories of mysterious lights at night were heard.

Queer Yarns

The thing went so far that it was related that Wigmore, the moving man, had found great difficulty in getting furniture out of the house. It was even told that pieces which had been placed in the moving van were found back in their place when the men re-ascended the stairs. The late James Wigmore, who was a boy when his father moved the Van Cortlandt furniture, and was present, when asked by O.T.S. about a year before his death, as to the truth of the stories said "All bosh. The stuff came out like any other furniture."

But anyway for many years the old house had the name of being haunted, and people who had to pass it at night hurried by.

Vacant Many Years

The house (as far as can be remembered) remained vacant till early in the nineties. The one bold person rented the so called "haunted" house, and opened a boarding house. As nothing happened to anything or anybody within a year, people ceased to regard the house as "haunted."

Was Busy Man

Dr. Van Cortlandt was, it might be mentioned, a coroner. He was also a consulting physician at the Protestant hospital. He was also attending physician at the Protestant House of Refuge on Wellington street near Bay.

There have been many doctors in Ottawa since Bytown times. Only a few names of the early doctors have survived, or are mentioned to any extent. It is safe to say that the name of Edward Van Cortlandt will be recalled for many years yet.

A Live Citizen

The doctor lived a very busy life. He was a live citizen. His name stood to the forefront at all public meetings, and all civic movements. Yes, he found time for study and research. Plainly put, Dr. "Van" was a remarkable man. As already told, he was regarded as eccentric. It is related that he had a very sensitive nature and was prone to take offence, where none was intended. He was quick tempered, but never held spite.

An Association

Dr. Van Cortlandt was peculiar to Wellington street. A story of Wellington street would not be complete without a story of the doctor. He lived and died there, and though the old home has gone, his name will always be associated with the street.

While this story is an interesting look at the manner by which the Van Cortlandt home was considered haunted, and then, over time, thought to be just a regular house, there are several other stories about the house scattered through the pages of the *Ottawa Citizen*.

One of them, from July 21, 1923, reveals the mystery behind the flickering lights.

One night, an Inspector Patrick Hanrahan was on late-night duty on Wellington street. Familiar with the odd stories being told about the allegedly haunted Van Cortlandt house, the inspector became intrigued when he spied for himself lights rising and dying out on the very top storey, the attic, of the vacant home.

As he stood watching the home, Hanrahan again saw the light reappear, flicker for a moment, then die off again.

He then walked up Sparks street where he found Constable Jos. Racine and brought him back to witness the eerie phenomenon. As the two stood on the street watching the home they noticed the light flickering again, similar to the way it had when Hanrahan had been watching the house on his own.

The two decided to investigate and, walking around the building, found that a back door of the house was unlocked. Ascending cautiously through the dark to the top floor, they discovered four vagrants stretched out on the floor and smoking.

Another mystery solved.

The Ghost of Ida Moore

Ida Moore died much too young, and the twenty-year-old's 1900 death prompted large groups of people to walk for miles in order to pay their respects at her funeral. But as the story goes, despite the fuss made by so many in order to properly lay her to rest, she never did lay at rest. Instead, she continues to wander around, playing mischievous tricks on those who dare go near the Moore House.

Originally built by J.P. Moore in 1850, on land provided to him by his father, William Moore, Moore created a home that he thought he might one day give to his daughter. Unfortunately, the beautiful young Ida, who demonstrated a talent for playing the piano and had a promising future, with plans to go to music school and become a teacher, contracted tuberculosis and died.

Ida was buried in a family cemetery plot on the outskirts of town, but many claim that though her body was laid to rest, her spirit remains animated and ever present, even to this day. Speculation abounds that the young woman's spirit was so angry with her fate that she remained in her beloved home and delighted in terrifying anyone who dared step inside.

Over the years, people entering the building have reported hearing strange noises, as well as noticing that objects have been regularly relocated seemingly on their own. Windows and doors have opened and closed all on their own and occasionally radios will be turned on or off by unseen hands.

Some say that Ida is not an angry spirit, but rather a playful and friendly one who enjoys playing tricks on those who cross the threshold into the house.

When the Moore family vacated the house, it became a general store. Legend has it that nobody who worked there wanted to be left alone, due to the tricks that Ida's ghost would play on them. It was also said that she had a particular penchant for playing tricks on the young men who walked through the doors.

In 2006, when the building was donated to the town of Carleton Place, the building was moved to its current location on 170 Bridge Street. During the move, a type of funeral walk, it was rumored that Ida was visible to some. "There were stories that when the house was being moved and coming down Bridge Street, you could see her ghost," said Catherine McOrmond of the Carleton Place BIA (Business in Action). Apparently Ida's ghost walked alongside the house and continues to reside in the new location on Bridge Street.

Stories continued to be shared about her ongoing exploits and tom-foolery. The sound of ghostly footsteps pacing the second floor, or heavy, loud footsteps coming down the stairs are heard by volunteers working in the heritage building.

In the fall of 2013, Ottawa-area writer Linda Seccaspina took a series of photos of the Moore House and noticed, in one of the pictures, a small orb floating just below the edge of the roof on the left hand side of the home's wall. She wondered if it might be Ida trying to pose for a picture.

While Ida continues to play tricks and make her presence felt, the townspeople of Carleton Place have continued to accept her presence. A concluding note about the Moore House on the Heritage Carleton Place website, which is sponsored and produced by the Municipal Heritage Committee of the Town of Carleton Place, says: "Every small town has a ghost story and this one is ours."

The Renfrew Lady and the Grabby-Clothes Ghost

It is interesting to come across ghost stories reported in local newspapers more than eighty years ago. They have both a sense of secretive whisper as well as a factual basis that makes them curious to behold and fascinating to share.

Below appears an intriguing case of a woman who experienced a ghost that seemed to be interested in items of worldly affect, such as this woman's bedclothes.

It appeared in an article in the *Ottawa Citizen* on January 31, 1931.

Clothes Pulled Off Bed By Ghostly Hands on Augusta St.
An Ottawa Ghost Story as Experienced by Renfrew Lady,
Bed Was Shaken Also. People of House Had Often Heard
People Walking in the House. A Peculiar Story.

Ghost stories have been a little scarce of late, but today another one has bobbed up. It is told by Mr. Alex Lepine of 64 Baywater avenue. This ghost story is an Ottawa ghost story.

Mr. Lepine tells that in the year 1909 or 1910 a lady from Renfrew came to visit a friend who lived on

Augusta street here. The house where she visited was near Anglesea Square.

Some time after the Renfrew lady has retired, she was awakened by the bed being shaken. At first she thought the shaking might have been occasioned by an earthquake.

She lay still for a time and listened. Again the bed was shaken, but as nothing else in the room appeared to have shaken the lady began to look for local causes.

A third time the bed was shaken and in a rather rough manner.

Clothes Pulled Off

But the worst was yet to come.

A minute later the lady felt the bedclothes being slowly but surely drawn off the bed. She grabbed the clothes to stay their going, but something stronger than herself continued the pull. That was too much. The Renfrew Lady let the clothes go and jumped from the bed and groped her way to the electric light, which she turned on. The light failed to reveal another in the room who could have shaken the bed or pulled the bedclothes. She left the light on the balance of the night.

Other Noises

The next day the Renfrew lady told her hostess about her experience and asked whether she had ever had a similar experience.

The hostess said she had never had just such an experience, but since they had been in the house, about six months, they had often heard sounds of someone walking in the house, and noises up in the attic or on the roof.

Wouldn't Stay

The Renfrew lady did not stay in the house the following night. She made an excuse and went to visit other friends.

Mr. Lepine says that he learned later that the people who lived in that house left when their year was up, as the strange noises had got on their nerves.

Mackenzie King
Speaking with Ghosts

The United States might have had their fair share of presidents having torrid and well-publicized extramarital affairs, or political cover-ups, such as the Watergate scandal, but how many can speak of a leader who spoke with the dead?

William Lyon Mackenzie King, Canada's tenth and longest-serving prime minister, was a practising spiritualist who attended séances, did experiments with Ouija boards, and regularly communed with spirits, including the spirits of family members, former Canadian leaders, and even dead U.S. presidents.

Mackenzie King was born on December 17, 1874, in Berlin, Ontario (now known as Kingston). His grandfather was William Lyon Mackenzie, the first mayor of the city of Toronto and leader of the Upper Canada Rebellion in 1837. King's father was a lawyer, and, despite never being financiallly secure, hired servants and tutors that the family could barely afford. King was tutored in math, science, politics, English, and French.

All of the extra learning at a young age seemed to have made an impression on the young man. King earned five university degrees and is the only prime minister to have earned a Ph.D.

In 1901, King's best friend and roommate, Henry Albert Harper, died after diving into icy waters of the Ottawa River in an attempt to save a young woman who fell through the ice during a skating party. King, who wrote about Harper as "the man I loved as I have loved no other man, my father and brother alone excepted," led the effort to raise a 1905 memorial to his dear friend, the erection of the only statue on Parliament Hill not portraying a politician or monarch. The statue, in honour of Henry Albert Harper, is of Sir Galahad. Both Mackenzie and Harper were fond of Alfred Tennyson's Arthurian works, and as he was diving into the icy waters, in response to those trying to dissuade a risky rescue attempt, Harper apparently quoted Galahad's famous line: "If I lose myself, I save myself."

His dearest friend is not the only person Mackenzie lost. His sister Bella died in 1915, followed by his father the very next year. His mother, who he was extremely devoted to, died in 1917, and his brother, Max, died in 1922.

King was a practising Presbyterian his entire life, and thus was predisposed by his faith to believe in the afterlife. That belief is likely what carried him through much of the grief that he experienced in such a condensed period of time.

He was considered a workaholic with a shrewd and sensitive handle on the temperament of the Canadian people. Therefore, when he began to become involved in spiritualism, he knew enough to keep his interest in communing with spirits of the dead and his contact and use of mediums secret and private. After all, with his religion condemning the consultation of fortune tellers or spirit guides and the people of Canada likely being suspicious of a leader consulting otherworldly entities, he knew enough not to mention that.

Mackenzie King kept a comprehensive diary, which he wrote in nearly every single day for a period of nearly fifty-seven years, from 1893 to 1950. In his diaries, a rich historical source of a first-person perspective of Canada and the world from Canada's longest-serving prime minister, which are available online, there are countless references to meetings with mediums over the years.

His exploits, however, were not known to the general public. It wasn't until about a year after his death that *Maclean's* magazine published an article by Blair Fraser entitled "Mackenzie King's Search for Survival," in which King's closet spiritualism first came to light.

Author C.P. Stacey, who called Mackenzie's diary "the most important single document in twentieth century Canadian history," was the first to examine the strange and obsessive drives behind the scenes while the man was in such a role of power, in his 1976 book *A Very Double Life: The Private World of Mackenzie King*.

In his diary entries, there is mention of a visit to a fortune teller as early as 1896, where Mackenzie King was impressed with what he had been told. He experienced a Syrian palm reader in Calgary in 1920, an aboriginal phrenologist and fortune teller in Atlantic City in 1915, and he attended a séance in 1925 in Kingston. He also spent some time with mediums in the 1930s in Kingston, Brockville, Ottawa, Toronto, and as far away as Winnipeg. But he became most involved as a spiritualist later in his life, typically when he was between periods of leadership.

Mackenzie King enjoyed looking for patterns in things such as tea leaves, or even the hands on a clock. He was certain that, if he glanced at a clock and the hands were perfectly aligned with the minute hand covering the hour hand, that it indicated some deeper significance in that moment.

King's meetings with Mrs. Rachel Bleaney between 1925 and 1930 allowed him to feel connected to the spirits of his dear mother and his brother, Max. In a lengthy diary entry, Mackenzie King noted almost everything she had said. He wrote that she "gave me a reading in the drawing room this afternoon, a truly remarkable experience…. It was amazingly true of the past and if true to the future will be astonishing beyond words, because so bold and daring in what it promised."

Mrs. Bleaney, however, left King with a series of predictions and statements that didn't hold true. She said he would win a general election that was coming soon (he lost to Arthur Meighen). She predicted that he would marry a widow in the next year and that the year, 1926, would be a good one for him. (King never married and 1926, the year of the lost election, was a particularly bad one for him.) She said he would live to be an old man of either seventy-eight or eighty years, but King died when he was seventy-five.

In 1932, Mackenzie King met Henrietta "Etta" Wreidt through a long-time friend, Mary Fulford. He attended séances at her home and also invited her to Ottawa, where she would conduct them at Laurier House, the Château Laurier, and at the estate at Kingsmere. He also visited her home in Detroit.

Among the various spirits that Wreidt helped Mackenzie King get in contact were his dear friend Albert Harper, his grandfather William Lyon Mackenzie (whom he was pleased to be able to wish a happy birthday to), and even his deceased dogs, which he loved dearly.

There are multiple references to conversations with spirits in the thousands of pages of Mackenzie King's diaries. Below are some excerpts from Mackenzie King's diary illustrating his involvement and the depths of his conviction for communing with the dead.

Thursday, June 30, 1932

Kingsmere. This day at Kingsmere was in some ways the best of all since Mrs. Wreidt came down. Joan and I had her wholly to ourselves and I was able to have a talk or two quite alone. What I really should have done, having reference to the greatness of this opportunity, was to have lived the week in prayer & writing out what was said immediately after the conversations. There can be no doubt whatsoever that the persons I have been talking with were the loved ones & others I had known and who had passed away. It was the spirits of the departed. There is no other way on earth of accounting for what we have all experienced this week. Just because it is *so* self-evident, it seems hard to believe. It is like those who had Christ with them in His day. Because it was all so simple, so natural, they would not believe & sought to destroy. I know whereof I speak, that nothing but the presence [of] those who have departed this life, but not this world, or vice versa could account for the week's experience.

The "conversations" in many cases have been so loud, so clear, etc. that I have felt great embarrassment at the servants in other parts of the house hearing what was said as I am sure they have. Mrs. Wreidt herself is a truly remarkable person, as enjoyable as a guest as I have known in my life, a person with so much of interest in her own life, so much to tell of the reality which lies behind the scene or apparent.

I have felt very tired during most of this week, through the presence of so many in the house, & not time sufficient to do as I would like to.

Friday, July 1, 1932

Kingsmere — Mrs. Wreidt leaves for Monteal. Mrs. Wreidt left at 3 this afternoon for Montreal. She was remarkably patient and appreciative up to the very end. I had little or nothing in the way of entertainment for her, nor did she seem to expect it, — with others present I had to divide time with them, which was a mistake as regards both them and her.

I figured out what seemed to be a generous allowance to make to her, meeting all of her travelling expenses in full and giving her the equivalent of $25 a day or for the books with which she has presented me. I also arranged to pay her fare to Montreal, so that she would be under no expense whatsoever.

She had brought many pretty little simple frocks etc. with her. I felt anxious lest she had exacted anything or much in the way of meeting people or entertainment. I don't think she did but she came prepared.

This anxiety for the comfort of one's guests, destroys much of what it might be possible to do & to enjoy. Every day, I see the great mistake made in not having married years ago, but as dear mother says "Marriage is a lottery" & it is a thousand times better not to be married at all than to be unhappily married.

> I have found the greatest relief to my mind & heart in all that mother & Bell & the others have said of Joan & their love for her. They understand, they know, and they are less harsh in judgement than the God we have invented for ourselves.
>
> I can see where the experiences of the past few days have changed somewhat my views on the life hereafter — prayer, God, etc. — but I believe it is all for the better, more rational, more the truth.

It must be noted, of course, that King was not alone in his interest and participation in spiritualism and communing with the dead. There was a movement of spiritualism throughout North America and around the world that begin in the 1850s and continued to grow. It continued to thrive in the wake of the First World War, as millions of grieving parents, siblings, wives, and children dealt with so much grief and were looking for ways to feel good about their loved ones having "passed on" to a better place. Illusionist and escape artist Harry Houdini, author Sir Arthur Conan Doyle, Queen Victoria, Napoleon, and even Mary Todd Lincoln (Abraham Lincoln's wife) were all known to have been involved in spiritualism.

A 1997 *Maclean's* magazine survey of scholars ended up ranking Mackenzie King first among all of Canada's prime ministers, ahead of such notable figures as Sir John A. Macdonald and Sir Wilfrid Laurier. While the scholars expressed little admiration for the man himself, their responses were filled with unbounded admiration for the man's political skills and attention to Canadian unity.

"Parliament will decide," he was known to say when pressed to comment or act upon popularly expressed opinions. "In times of need, all nations face difficult decisions, Canada is not an exception."

The Spooky Ruins of Mackenzie King

There is a country estate in Gatineau Park known as Kingsmere. In 1934, Mackenzie King began to collect architectural ruins from various locations all over the world and assembling them into beautiful and picturesque "ruins." These include the Abbey, the Cloisters (one of his most industrious undertakings), the Chapel, and the Temple. These ruins included elements such as a curved window from the Ottawa home of Simon-Napoleon Parent (premier of Quebec from 1900 to 1905), stones from the ruins of the original Canadian Parliament Buildings, which were destroyed by fire in 1916, and a shield and a fireplace from the Speaker's chamber in the British Houses of Parliament at Westminster.

Mackenzie King died on the estate in July 22, 1950, and bequeathed it to all Canadians as "a public park in trust for the people of Canada." The park, now 231 hectares in size, is a part of Gatineau Park, the National Capital Region's conservation park.

While the ruins themselves are beautiful, they are also spooky and eerie to behold.

Considering that Mackenzie King used to conduct séances in which he would speak to spirits of the departed, and writer Philip J. Percy relayed a story of actually speaking with the ghost of the former prime minster on those grounds, many believe that the location must be haunted.

Haunted Walks Inc. tours of the Mackenzie King Estate in the Gatineau Hills are popular as there are many intriguing historic tales to share.

Courtesy of Haunted Walks Inc.

In a story relayed in John Robert Colombo's book *Ghost Stories of Canada*, poet Gwendolyn MacEwan shared an experience that still, as she says, "chills her blood."

MacEwan was visiting Ottawa in the early 1960s to recite poetry. When the reading event was over, her host offered to take her to Kingsmere in order to see the ruins. Though it was getting late and dark, they thought it would be a fun adventure.

They reached the estate just before midnight, parked the car, and had begun walking toward the ruins when rain began to fall and a thunderstorm began, with bright flashes of lightning that completely lit up the ruins of the estate.

The two ran forward in an effect to stay out of the rain, but another bright lighting strike illuminated the ruins right in front of them and what they saw froze them completely in their tracks.

There, in arch of the Chapel, stood a glowing human figure.

"Did you see that?" MacEwan's host asked her.

"I don't want to talk about it," she replied.

They both then raced back through the rain to their car and didn't speak for most of the long ride home.

MacEwan shared the experience many years later, in 1987, shortly before she died.

Speaking with
Mackenzie King's Ghost

In the preceding chapters, we looked at William Lyon Mackenzie King's penchant for spiritualism, the mostly secret obsession he had with communing with the dead. Public knowledge of the man's consultation with mediums and attending séances, of his belief in fortune-telling and palmistry wasn't revealed in any big way until 1976, when C.P. Stacey released his 1976 book *A Very Double Life: The Private World of Mackenzie King*.

But well before that, in 1954, another writer brought Mackenzie into a "ghostly" light.

Writer Percy J. Philip, a notable war correspondent who Mackenzie had on his shortlist of favourite newsmen, paid a visit to Kingsmere, the Gatineau Hills estate just north of Ottawa, two years after King had died. While on the estate he sat on a bench and engaged in a conversation with the late former prime minister.

The following is an excerpt from the December 1995 issue of *Fate* magazine.

> On a June evening in 1954 I had a long conversation with the former Canadian Prime Minister William L. Mackenzie King as we sat on a bench in the grounds of his old summer home at Kingsmere, 12 miles from

Ottawa. It seemed to me an entirely normal thing although I knew perfectly well that Mr. King had been dead for four years.

Of course, when I returned to Ottawa and told my story nobody quite believed me. I myself became just the least bit uncertain as to whether it really had happened, or at least as to how it had happened. Did I fall asleep and dream? Was this due to paranormal circumstances which cannot be explained?

Of one thing I am sure. Mr. King himself would believe me. He once held similar conversations — almost daily in some cases — with persons who had left this world. He talked with his father and mother regularly and with great men and women of the past. His diary, in which he recorded his spiritual experiences, as well as his political activities and contacts, gives detailed accounts of these conversations. Unfortunately it is not likely to be published in full because his will provided that certain parts should be destroyed. His literary executors feel bound to carry out these instructions.

It was not until after his death that the Canadian people learned that their bachelor, liberal Prime Minister communed with the dead both directly and, occasionally, through mediums. When it did become known — in a rather sensational way — it shocked many.

Yet the Prime Minister made no secret of his beliefs and practices. To friends who had lost dear ones he wrote in this manner: "I know how you feel. It seems as though you cannot bear to go on without that wonderful companionship and affection. But let me assure you that love still exists. A bond as strong as that is not broken by death or anything else. Your father is still near you. If you can be still and listen and feel, you will realize he is close to you all your life. I know that because it is so with my mother and me."

That quotation is from one of the many hundreds of letters of condolence which Mr. King wrote with his own hand for he was punctilious in such matters. At funerals he always spoke similar words of comfort to those bereaved. Otherwise, although he made no secret of his beliefs, he did not parade them.

Once, at Government House, about Christmas time in 1945, he told the Governor General, the Earl of Athlone, that he had spoken with President Roosevelt the previous night. "President Truman, you mean," said the Governor. The Earl saw that some of his staff were making signs from behind Mr. King's back, evidently trying to convey some message. He was puzzled but, being a good constitutional Governor General, he kept quiet and did not again correct the Prime Minister when he repeated, "Oh, no, I mean the late President Roosevelt."

The occasion of the incident was the showing of the Noël Coward film, "Blithe Spirit," which Mr. King found "most interesting."

"It is difficult to imagine the life after death," he said, chatting gaily. "Probably the best thing to do is to regard it as a continuation of the one we know with the same processes of growth and change until, eventually, we forget our life and associations on this earth, just as old people tend to forget their childhood experiences."

His Excellency who was a brother of the late Queen Mary and a soldier by profession muttered, "Yes, yes, probably." He obviously was shaken. He had been chosen by Mr. King to be Governor General of Canada and it made him nervous to learn that his Prime Minister was receiving advice from extra-mundane sources.

"Good God," he exclaimed when his staff explained why they had tried to shush him, "is that where the man gets his policies?"

Having an open mind about the occult and being inquisitive by nature, I later managed to turn several conversations with Mr. King to this subject. Once, especially, when we were crossing the Atlantic to Europe, he talked freely about his beliefs and experiences as we walked the deck.

"If one believes in God and a life after death," he said, "it is inevitable that one must believe that the spirits of those who have gone take an interest in the people and places they loved during their lives on earth. It is the matter of communication that is difficult. For myself I have found that the method of solitary, direct, communion is best. After my father and mother died I felt terribly alone. But I also felt that they were near me. Almost accidentally I established contact by talking to them as if they were present and soon I began to get replies."

These and other things that the Prime Minister said to me at different times came back to my mind as, on that June evening, I drove up the Kingsmere road and was reminded by a sign that the estate of Moorside, which Mr. King had left to the Canadian people in his will, lay just ahead.

It is a beautiful place. There are 550 acres of woodland and clearings, through most of which everyone is free to wander at will. A little stream with a waterfall flows through it down to the valley below. Mr. King accumulated it almost acre by acre, adding steadily in his methodical way, to the original lot he had bought when he first came to Ottawa at the beginning of the century. His quick temper seldom flashed more hotly than when he discovered that some neighbour had sold a parcel of land without giving him a chance to buy. Adding to his estate became a passion with the future Prime Minister. There he loved to receive visitors and also to be alone.

In buying the land Mr. King showed his Scottish shrewdness. But the building of the "ruins" was a perfect example of that romantic daftness that sometimes bewitches the supposedly hard-headed Scot. The direction sign now set up for tourists calls them "ruins" but the uninformed must wonder what they once were. There were doorways and windows, a fireplace, a row of columns, which Mr. King called the cloisters, coats of arms carved in stone, bits and pieces of the old Parliament Buildings, the mint, banks and private houses all built into an artistic enough wholly whimsical suggestion of a ruined castle. Somehow, perhaps because the surroundings with outcrop rock and pine are so fitting, they escape being silly.

On that evening there were no other visitors. The air was clear and cool. I sat down on a bench beside the ruins and thought about the strange little man who loved his hill-top home so dearly. I suppose I was in what I called a receptive mood. Although I had not then read it, I was following the instructions in that letter from which I already have quoted, to "be still and listen and feel."

I became conscious that I was not alone. Someone sat on the park bench beside me.

There were no sighs, groans and lightning flashes such as mark a spirit's arrival on the Shakespearian stage. There was, if anything, a deeper peace. Through a fold in the hills I could see a stretch of the broad Ottawa Valley. I tried to concentrate on it and keep contact with the normal but the presence on the bench would not be denied.

Without turning my head, for somehow I feared to look, I said as naturally as I could, "Good evening, Mr. King."

In that warm tone which always marked his conversation the voice of Mr. King replied, "Good evening, Philip. I am so glad you spoke to me."

That surprised me. "I was thinking of you," I muttered.

"Oh, yes," he replied. "I knew that. But one of the rules which govern our conduct on this side is that we are like the children and must not speak unless we are spoken to. I suppose it is a good rule because it would be very disturbing if we went around talking to people. The sad thing is that so few of them ever talk to us."

Here I think I should say that the reader must decide for himself whether or not he believes this story. It puzzles me greatly.

"I suppose," I said, or I think I said, resuming the conversation, "that we are just a bit scared. You know how hard it is to speak into a dark, empty room."

"That certainly is a difficulty for many people," Mr. King said. "But the room is never really empty. It is often filled with lonely ones who would like to be spoken to. They must, however, be called by name, confidently, affectionately, now challenged to declare themselves."

"Your name," I said, "must often be so mentioned in this lovely place you bequeathed to the Canadian people."

"Oh, yes, mentioned," he said. I glanced at him and seemed to see his eyes sparkle as they did in life, for he had a great deal of puckish humor. "But between being mentioned and being addressed by name, as you addressed me, there is a great deal of difference. I have heard things about my character, motives, political actions and even my personal appearance and habits that have made me laugh so loudly I thought I must break the sound barrier. And I have heard things about myself, too, that have made me shrink."

In the evening silence I had the sensation of being suspended in time and space as the quiet voice went on. "There are things that I said and did that I could regret but, on this side, we soon learn to have no regrets. Life would be meaningless if we did not all make mistakes, and eternity intolerable if we spent it regretting them."

He paused and I thought he looked at me quizzically. "By the way," he said, "Do you still write for the *New York Times*?"

When I said that I had retired, he chuckled. "But still," he said, "I think I had better not give indiscreet answers to your questions."

I asked several but he answered with the same skill as marked his replies to questions in the House of Commons and at meetings with the press, divulging nothing. It was I who was the interviewed. He was eager for news and it surprised me then, as it does now, that he seemed not to know fully what was happening in the world. The dead, I discovered, are not omniscient. Or perhaps what we think important is not important to them.

We talked of the development of Canada, of housing and new enterprises like the St. Lawrence Seaway. "My successor has been lucky," Mr. King said. That was as far as he went in any personal reference. "Canada has been very prosperous. I hope it will continue to be so. But you cannot expect good times always. It is adversity that proves the real value of men and nations."

The conversation drifted to the international scene, to philosophic discussion of forms of government, of the balance between Liberty and Authority, the growth and decay of nations and of systems. I cannot tell how long it lasted but I noticed that the sickle moon was getting brighter. I mentioned the time, fumbling for my watch.

"Time," said Mr. King, "I had almost forgotten about time. I suppose I spend a great deal of time up here. There is so much beauty and peace. I gave it to the Canadian people but in a way I have preserved it for myself. It is good to have some familiar, well-loved place to spend 'time' in, until one gets used to eternity."

We both rose from the bench — or at least I did. When I looked at him, as I then did for the first time directly, he seemed just as I had known him in life, just as when I had talked with him once at this very spot.

"I think you told me once that you are Scottish born and a wee bit 'fey,' " he said. "It's a good thing to be. We have two worlds. Those people who think their world is the only one, and who take it and themselves too seriously, have a very dull time. Do come back and talk with me again."

I muttered words of thanks and then, following the habit of a lifetime, stretched out my hand to bid goodbye. He was not there.

Chichester Ghost of Ottawa River

Ghosts are often seen as spectral forms continually repeating the same action over and over for all of eternity — trapped in the hell of going through the exact same motions. Then, just as quickly as they seemed to materialize out of nothing, they fade away and are seen no more. Is this because whatever it was that trapped them in this eternal replay was resolved, or was some other need met, allowing them to move on?

The following report is taken from an *Ottawa Citizen* article dated April 19, 1929.

As an aside, it is interesting to not just enjoy the tale as it was originally told, but to pay attention to the way that the writer draws specific attention to the fact it is a written tale. Not often in modern journalism does the narrative flow purposely make the reader stop and remember that they are reading a story.

Chichester Ghost Was Sensation; Spirit Drowned Man Seen Often

Walked the River Road to Chichester, Moaned and Reenacted Accident Which Caused His Death — Seen and Heard by Scores — Haunted Scene for Several Years, Then Disappeared.

The material which follows constitutes a more or less certified ghost story. It involves an "appearance," moans and all the paraphernalia of a real ghost story.

The locale of this ghost story is laid between the bridge over the Ottawa river near Chapeau and the village of Chichester where the Poupores used to have their big saw mills and stores. The date was about 1875 and the story is narrated by Mr. Thos. Donoher, of 208 Main Street, Ottawa East.

It appears that in the fall of 1874 a man had been drowned in the Ottawa river about a mile west of the bridge, and on the way to Chichester — that is on the Quebec side of the river. Between the bridge end and Chichester the road runs about an acre back from the river, and at the point where the drowning took place the river was in full view from the road.

The Tragedy

So that what follows will be best understood, it should be told that the victim of the drowning had lost his life by falling into the river while trying to get a drink from a fairly steep bank.

Now, dear reader, wake up, the ghost is about to appear.

Ghost Appears

The following spring (1875) a woman who drove one evening from Chapeau to Chichester reported that she had seen a ghostly form standing on the bank of the river

74

just where the man of the story had lost his life, and as she looked the apparition stooped down as though to drink, and then fell forward into the water and disappeared. In other words the tragedy had been reenacted.

Soon after that, the apparition was seen by others walking on the road. Reports came of horses being violently excited and of their refusing to move till the apparition had gone out of sight.

Horse Bolted

In one case, when the ghost appeared suddenly on the road, a short distance from a horse, the animal bolted, throwing the driver out and running over two miles into Chichester, arriving there foam-covered.

Heard Moans

People who did not see an apparition averred and swore that they had distinctly heard moans on the road near the scene of the drowning.

Came To Be Habit

The ghost became a habit, as it were, and before the winter set in many people who had to drive on the Chichester road, either way, at night saw the apparition — or swore they did — which was the same thing in effect.

In due time the ghost came to be known as the "Chichester Ghost" and was firmly believed in by hundreds.

The ghost haunted that road for several years, but ceased to appear after the Chichester road had the bush cut from its sides.

A Theory

It might be mentioned in this connection that there were people on Allumette Island (who were possibly sore at the ghost not being an island ghost) who averred that the moans that were heard were the noise of tree boughs rubbing against each other, but they could not quite explain away the apparition, which many of their own people swore to have seen.

Such is the story of the Chichester ghost! Believe what you like.

The Ghost of Watson's Mill

"Sometimes, when a dramatic death occurs and there is a lot of grief, it's almost as if a building picks up all these vibrations, the same as a record picks up the vibrations of the singers," Dr. Beverly Janus of the Institute of Parapsychology Studies said in an interview on the Canadian television series *Creepy Canada*, "If someone who is a receiver and highly open to the psychic comes into a place where a traumatic event occurred, they become almost like the needle."

Many "receivers" have passed through Watson's Mill, an historic grist mill located in Manotick, just twenty-five kilometres south of downtown Ottawa. The only working museum in the National Capital Region and one of a very few operating industrial grist mills in North America, Watson's Mill continues to sell stone-ground whole-wheat flour made right on the site. With its image being used as a symbol for the village, which has a population of approximately 4,500 people, it has become Manotick's most recognized landmark, is open to the public during the summer and hosts an ongoing calendar of events.

Built by Moss Kent Dickinson and his partner, Joseph Currier, in 1860, the mill, originally known as Long Island Flouring Mills, is older than Canada itself. Dickinson, who also founded the town of Manotick, branded it with that name after the Algonquin word for "island in the river."

The power of the river is the prime driver of a mill's operation, and the location of the forty-six-by-sixty-four-foot mill, built from the riverbed limestone, made it a central part of the village community. The foundation walls were constructed four feet thick at the base and narrowed by six inches at each level going up. Multiple architectural journals have described the mill as being one of the best examples of nineteenth-century grist-mill architecture.

The Dickinsons operated the mill until Aleck Spratt bought it in 1929. For the majority of the time that Aleck and his wife, Evelyn, owned the mill, Henry Watson worked there. Aleck Spratt died in 1935 and Watson eventually bought it from Evelyn in 1946. One of the first things that Watson did when purchasing the mill was erect a sign over the front door, declaring it "Watson's Mill." That name has continued, even after Watson sold the mill in 1972 to the Rideau Valley Conservation Authority, who took it upon themselves to restore one run of millstones and machinery to the original 1860 operating condition. Interestingly, the Authority hired Robert Watson, son of Henry, to retool the large water turbines that power the mill. The mill is still owned by the Rideau Valley Conservation Authority but is managed by Watson's Mill Manotick Inc., a volunteer, non-profit group.

On March 11, 1861, around the first anniversary of the mill's successful operation, owners Dickinson and Currier held a celebration at the mill. Currier used that occasion to introduce his second wife, and bride of just over a month, Ann Crosby Currier, the twenty-year-old daughter of a successful hotel owner from Caldwell, New York, to the mill. During their walk-through Currier was showing his new wife the moving equipment and machinery, when Dickinson and a few others distracted him away to discuss business. Because Currier and his wife had just returned from their honeymoon, there was a bit of catching up to do. So Currier excused himself from Ann and went off for an informal business meeting while she continued to wander and explore the second floor.

That is when tragedy struck.

Ann's crinoline and dress became caught in a revolving turbine shaft on the second floor and the force of the machinery threw her hard against a support pillar, striking her head. The violent and sudden nature of this trauma killed her instantly.

Shocked and devastated by the loss of his wife, Joseph Currier sold his shares in the business to Dickinson and left Manotick, never wanting to return to the town again. Returning his attention to the lumber and construction business as a way to get over the tragic loss of his dear newlywed bride, Currier threw himself into his work. This re-engagement saw him achieve such positions as president of Citizen Printing and Publishing Company (publishers of the *Ottawa Citizen*), president of two different railway companies, a representative for Ottawa in the Legislative Assembly of the Province of Canada, and postmaster of Ottawa. Just as historic as the mill he built with Moss Kent Dickinson was the official residence of the prime minister of Canada, which Currier built in 1868 as a wedding gift for his third wife, Hannah. Currier christened the house "Gorffwysfa," which is a Welsh term meaning "place of peace."

Currier was able to build a new life and escape from the tragic loss of his beloved Ann, but his departed bride was not so lucky.

"This is a highly charged story about emotion — raw emotion called love," Terry Boyle, author of the book *Haunted Ontario* and host of the television program *Creepy Canada,* said. "Unfortunately this love would and wouldn't extend beyond the grave. She's still there. He may not be. Love has kept her chained to the place she died."

The first reported encounter with the ghost occurred in 1920, when a fisherman was fishing off the dam at Watson's Mill and was caught in a violent wind-and-rain storm. Seeking shelter, he climbed in through an open basement window of the mill, where he took refuge for the night. Safe and protected from the storm, the fisherman fell asleep inside the building while listening to the howling winds outside. In the middle of the night he was awakened by a different sound: the unearthly sound of a woman crying. He remained on the first floor, absolutely terrified by the sounds of weeping and moaning that he heard from upstairs. But he remained huddled in his spot, curious about who might also be seeking refuge. In the morning light, he quietly found his way upstairs to find that he had been the only person inside the building.

Many people living in the village of Manotick have reported seeing what they believe to be the ghost of Ann Currier moving from window to window on the second floor of the building long after the museum has been closed for the night. Some report that the woman they spotted was dressed in old-fashioned clothing and others report that she appears to be very sad as she looks down and out the window at them.

"Many residents say they've seen Anna Currier's ghost in the window," historian Laurie Moodie told the *Ottawa Citizen* for a 1986 article. "We've had reports of a shadow seen at night, but no one is supposed to be in the mill at night."

One quiet evening in 1980, a pair of local schoolboys reported that they were walking across the dam when they spotted a shadowy spectre in one of the second-floor windows. Frozen in terror, they said that the female ghost looked very mournful as it gazed down upon them.

During a *CTV Morning Live* taping at Watson's Mill in October 2011, reporter Melissa Lamb was startled on camera by an odd scratching noise at the exact spot that Ann Currier died. A few minutes later one of the cameras inexplicably went into auto-save mode for absolutely no reason at all just when they were filming and talking about one of the windows that Ann's ghost was regularly reported being seen in.

Watson's Mill employee Adam Moore said he had heard that Ann likes things to be done properly and that treating her with respect is important.

Actor Susan Murphy was cast to be the ghost of Watson's Mill in a documentary about the mill that was airing on a local cable station. Part of the role involved wearing a large gown and moving quietly down the stairs from the loft in a gliding and ghost-like manner. During the second take for that scene, just as Murphy was waiting for the director to give her the cue, she saw an eerie bluish haze swirl about the room, reflecting off the walls, following by an incredibly cold blast of air that felt like it went right through her. When, a few seconds later, the director gave her the cue she had been waiting for, Murphy says that she appeared, literally, as white as a ghost.

Visiting psychics have claimed that Ann Currier's ghost might not be the only one haunting the mill and that there are perhaps other presences — several male presences — lingering on the third floor. Unlike Ann's morbidly weeping and forlorn spirit, these other presences are said to be more hostile and malevolent in nature. Reports of heavy footsteps and male voices coming from the vacant third floor have been reported, as well as heavy objects having inexplicable being moved when nobody was around.

When Glen Shackleton and a group of Haunted Walk tour guides spent the night in the mill in 2007 as part of an informal ghost investigation, a pair of investigators experienced something related to these male ghosts. Before the overnight investigation, Shackleton ensured that the descriptive panels appearing on the second floor, describing the tragedy and some of those reported stories about Ann's ghost, were covered up so as not to bias the investigators who were not familiar with the tales about the building.

With just the glow of a flashlight, the investigators entered the building in pairs and wandered about. Most of them reported feeling nothing other than damp, the occasional creak of the old building settling, and the dull roar of the river moving underneath. But one pair, wandering about the second floor, were frozen in their tracks when they both heard the distinct sound of male voices coming from the third floor.

While they could not make out any specific words, they said the intent of the voices was obvious: something on the third floor was angered by their presence and wanted them to leave.

In an interview with CTV reporter Melissa Lamb, Watson's Mill employee Adam Moore relayed the story of a lady who had seen the silhouette of a man on the third floor, which had frightened her terribly. "You don't really like to spend much time up here," Moore said.

While it's not known who the ghost or ghosts on the third floor could be, some speculate it might be Joseph Currier, returned to the mill after his own death and angered at having been separated from Ann in the last moments of her life. Others, including Glen Shackleton, speculate that the male spirits on the third floor could be those of workers who lost their lives in the mill over the years.

Cam Truman, education and interpretation officer for Watson's Mill, shared the story of when he and his brother-in-law, who was visiting from Winnipeg, had gone to the mill for a private tour. During the tour, Cam's brother-in-law took a series of photographs and they both enjoyed the experience. A couple of months later, Cam's brother-in-law showed him the pictures. There was a particularly large orb in one of the pictures taken of the third floor. Cam remarked that the orb was quite interesting, and speculated on whether or not it might just be the odd capture of light reflecting off a particular mote of dust in the air. However, when they flipped to the next picture, which was of the very same location but from a completely different angle, the orb appeared in exactly the same location it had appeared in the first picture.

Over the years reports from staff members have included numerous sightings of the ghost of Ann flitting from window to window, and the sound of eerie footsteps and wailing, as well as inexplicable temperature changes.

One particular afternoon, a female employee heard voices coming from the basement. She had never heard any stories of ghostly encounters from anywhere other than the second and third floors, so she went down to see if perhaps some visitors to the museum had wandered down there. When she got downstairs, she couldn't see anybody. There were no lights on and it was dark. But from the darkness she heard the rattling of chains. She also felt the temperature immediately drop. She rushed back up the stairs and avoided going back to the basement from that point forward.

While there appear to be multiple presences lingering in the building, the one most spoken about and most often seen is that of Ann Crosby Currier. Tales continue to be shared about her ghostly image peering out from the second-floor windows, forever reminding people of the tragic accident that took her young life.

While not everybody who visits the building sees or hears something, it could be that there are those who are more attuned to the vibrations left in that location, waiting to be uncovered by those possessing the ability to feel them.

As Dr. Beverly Janus told *Creepy Canada*, "It's not necessarily that there's a ghost living in the place, it's just that perhaps the event was seeped and recorded into the walls."

The Caretaker's Favourite Spot

Reg Hartt, a film archivist born in Rothwell, New Brunswick, and living in Toronto, has become well-known for the talks that he gives prior to film screenings, which he's been holding at rented locations, such as the Bathurst Street Church and the Spadina Hotel, since 1965. Since 1992, Hartt has shown films in the forty-seat theatre he has dubbed The Cineforum in his home on Barthurst Street in Toronto. The front window has a neon sign that reads "Cineforum," and there is a sign in Greek that reads "Abandon hope, all ye who enter here."

In Hartt's privately printed memoirs, which are excerpted in John Robert Colombo's *Ghost Stories of Ontario*, there is a tale involving a ghost that occurred in Ottawa in the 1960s.

While browsing through an Anglican bookstore, Hartt had picked up a few books on the subject of the occult. When he was ringing the books out the cashier commented on them and mentioned that, if he was interested, there was a group meeting that night who were studying that very subject.

Hartt found himself attending a meeting of the Bartonian Metaphysical Society. He sat in the back of the room, where he was able to maintain a comprehensive view, not just of the speaker but of the entire group seated there.

A woman by the name of Dr. Winnifred Barton stood in front of the crowd and spoke for about an hour. During her talk, Hartt scanned the room, checking out the crowd.

Hartt's eyes fell upon a man in a red plaid shirt. As soon as the man noticed that Harrt was looking at him, he faded away to nothing, right before his eyes. Throughout Dr. Barton's talk, Hartt kept scanning the room. He saw the man fade a couple more times before the intermission.

During the break, Hartt made a point of introducing himself to Dr. Barton and told her what he had witnessed while she was talking. She left the room and returned a moment later holding a photograph. She held it out to show it to Hartt, asking if he recognized the man in the picture.

"Yes, that's the man," Harrt said.

"That's the caretaker," Barton said, indicating the area that Hartt had seen him. "That was his favourite spot.

"He died yesterday."

Luxury and Tragedy at the Château Laurier

Mary Bellingham and her husband had already experienced a series of odd and unexplainable phenomenon in the first couple of nights after they'd checked in to Ottawa's premier luxury hotel, but it wasn't until the morning when she was alone in the shower, enjoying the feel of the hot water splashing against her skin, that she knew for sure the hotel must be haunted.

Mary and her husband, Frank, (not their real names) had arrived in Ottawa expecting to enjoy some time exploring the city from a central location. The Château Laurier was in the ideal spot, after all — nestled across the Rideau Canal from the Parliament Buildings and in the veritable heart of the downtown area, a quick walk to the local market and a handful of museums. It was a time for relaxing and exploring, enjoying each other's company as well as all of the variety and culture that the National Capital Region has to offer.

They had not heard any of the stories about the building or its ghosts, but when they left Mary knew that something unseen was definitely making its presence felt there. Frank did not experience anything. The spirit that lurked in their midst seemed to focus its energy and reveal its presence only to Mary.

It started off in a very unobtrusive fashion, but over time the presence became stronger and stronger.

Author's collection.

The Fairmount Château Laurier.

The first time, Mary had been alone in the suite, unpacking their clothes and humming to herself, while Frank had returned downstairs to retrieve something from their car. Mary suddenly became overwhelmed by a sensation of uneasiness. It had felt almost as if she was no longer alone. She paused to look over her shoulder and around the room, wondering if perhaps Frank had returned. But he wasn't there. She was still alone. So when she felt something brush against her arm, it sent a chill down her spine.

She brushed at her arm, confused, and continued unpacking.

Then the sensation happened again. A light passing touch crossing her arm, raising a wave of goose bumps on her flesh.

She paused, looked around again, saw nothing was there, and continued unpacking.

Nothing further happened at that point. A few minutes later Frank returned. They finished unpacking and they went about their normal travel routine.

The following night, at the end of a fun day spent exploring the city, Mary was preparing for bed when the second incident occurred. She was sitting in front of a large mirror by her dresser and removing makeup, when she thought she detected movement.

Sure enough, in the reflection of the mirror, she watched in shocked amazement as the closet door slowly opened all on its own.

The full day of city exploration and the chilling incident that had unsettled both Mary and her husband, after she relayed what she had seen to him, made for a very restless and anxious night.

So the following morning, while she stood in the shower, the feeling of the hot water cascading over her tired body was a welcome and much-needed repose. Her eyes closed and the spray from the shower splashing directly into her face, Mary let out a huge sigh of contentment. And that's when she felt the distinct feeling of a hand pressing up against her shoulder blade.

Unlike the soft and gentle brushing she had felt a couple of days earlier, there was no mistaking this for anything else. She had definitely felt a hand pressing up against her naked flesh.

And Frank was definitely not in the bathroom with her.

Shortly after, Mary and Frank contacted the folks from Haunted Walks Inc. and shared their story. It was then that they learned this beautiful and elegant building has been known not just for its charm and majesty, and not just for some unique ghostly tales, but also for its link to one of the best-known tragedies of the modern era.

The Fairmont Château Laurier, which is located at the intersection of Sussex Drive and Rideau Street and overlooks both the Ottawa River and the Rideau Canal locks, is a 429-room, 660,000-square-foot hotel. Declared a National Historic Site in 1981, the French Gothic style effectively matches the smooth granite blocks, the Indiana limestone, and the turreted copper roofs of the adjacent Parliament Buildings.

Commissioned by Charles Melville Hays, president of Grand Trunk Railway, the hotel was built in conjunction with the downtown Union Station (originally Ottawa's railway station, now the Government Conference Centre) directly across the street, between 1909 and 1912. With lobby floors constructed of Belgian marble and featuring original

Tiffany stained-glass windows and hand-moulded plastic décor, the hotel was built for two million dollars.

Though the design, construct, and architecture of the building were grand and elaborate, there was quite a degree of controversy surrounding the construction. There were those who were not at all happy with the new development. Citizens were concerned that the hotel's location would be a detriment to the natural beauty of Major's Hill Park. However, Prime Minister Wilfrid Laurier helped secure the site for construction, and the hotel was eventually named in his honour.

The proposed tunnels designed to connect the hotel to the railway station being built simultaneously across the street were met with fear and concern, due to the belief that the tunnels, with their lack of ventilation, would pose a health hazard, attract pickpockets, and, according to Glen Shackelton, "gentlemen whose misdemeanors were of a far more serious nature." Near the beginning of the project, the original architect for the hotel, Bradford Gilbert, fell into disagreement with Grand Trunk Railway executives and was dismissed; he was replaced by architects from the Montreal based firm of Ross and MacFarlane.

After four years of construction, the hotel was to be officially opened on April 26, 1912. In early April, owner Charles Melville Hays was in London attending meetings at Grand Trunk Railway's head office, and had booked a trip back to Canada aboard the maiden voyage of a brand new luxury steamship. Invited by fellow businessman J. Bruce Ismay, chairman of the White Star line, Hays, his wife, his daughter, his son-in-law, his secretary, and their maid shared a deluxe suite on the promenade deck of the ocean liner. The opulent and luxurious ship must have been, in the eyes of Hays, a fitting vessel to convey him to the grand opening of what was certain to become Ottawa's premier luxury hotel.

Unfortunately for Hays and the 1,500 other passengers and crew who perished in the early hours of April 15, 1912, in the frigid cold waters of the North Atlantic, the ship, which was the largest passenger liner in service at the time, was the ill-fated RMS *Titanic*.

On the tragic night in question, Hays hastily escorted his wife, daughter, and their maid onto one of the twenty lifeboats. Hays, his secretary, and son-in-law remained on the ship, where Hays allegedly assured the

Der Untergang der Titanic engraving by Willy Stöwe for *Die Gartenlaube* magazine, 1912.

females from his party that it would take at least ten hours for the ship to sink and there was plenty of time for those remaining on the ship to be rescued. Earlier that same evening, Hays reportedly stated that, due to the speed at which companies were racing to win over passengers by building faster and larger ships, "the time will come soon when this trend will be checked by some appalling disaster."

A ship called the *Minia* recovered Hays's body a few days later, and he was buried in the Mount Royal Cemetery in Montreal, with newspapers eulogizing his loss by citing him as one of the greatest railwaymen in Canada. Work on the Grand Trunk Railway was stopped for five minutes on April 25, 1912, in his memory, and his grand hotel, which was supposed to originally be opened as part of a celebration on April 26th, ended up being opened in June of that year at a subdued ceremony.

Over the past century, the Château Laurier has played host to debutantes, politicians, and celebrities from around the world, from royalty, such as Queen Elizabeth and Diana Princess of Wales, and politicians, such as Winston Churchill and Dwight Eisenhower, to rock stars, such as

John Lennon and the Rolling Stones. Due to its proximity to Parliament Hill, many politicians and heads of state stay there, and it became known in some circles as the "third chamber of Parliament." Prime Minister R.B. Bennett lived in a suite specifically designed for him. And during the First and Second World Wars the hotel was used for secret meetings between military leaders and powerful industrialists. In August of 1914 Major Raymond Brutinel enrolled the first recruits for the Canadian Automobile Machine Gun Brigade in the locale. Between 1924 and 2004 the two top floors, the seventh and the eighth, were home to the Canadian Broadcast Corporation's local English- and French-language radio stations. Yousuf Karsh, the world-famous Armenian-Canadian portrait photographer who took photographs of many of the dignitaries who visited the Château, held his first solo exhibition in 1936 in the Drawing Room there, and held his studio there from 1973 to 1992.

But, despite all of the famous people who have visited and stayed at the Château, there is one presence there that seems to carry far more weight.

Charles Melville Hays, who fought so hard to realize the dream of building something truly great, never got a chance to fulfill his dream of seeing the Château Laurier be the first of a chain of world-class luxury hotels. Many believe that although he never made it back for the grand opening in physical form, his spirit returned to the hotel and, in an odd combination of pride and sadness, continues to roam the halls and rooms of the hotel, never properly at peace.

In 1930, the hotel added an Art Deco style sixty-foot indoor pool as well as an adjacent spa, in which electroshock therapy was used to treat nervous afflictions. Considering that electroshock therapy has been used as a form of torture in war and by oppressive regimes, as a way to cause bursts of pain and fear in a person without leaving any physical evidence on the body, it isn't hard to imagine the echoes of those shocks remaining in the building's structure.

Among the various tales shared about ghostly encounters at the Château Laurier, the one that stands out and is most often shared involves Patrick Watson, who was serving as chairman of the CBC,

Author's collection.

The beautiful and elegant hallways of the Château Laurier can take on a more sinister feel in the middle of the night, especially after reading tales about the various bumps in the night experienced in some of the rooms.

which operated their radio station from the seventh and eighth floors of the hotel for over sixty-eight years.

Watson, who had been staying in one of the hotel suites in the 1980s, was awoken one night by what he believed was the sound of a pistol. He immediately sat up in bed, a chill running down his spine, as his eyes tried to penetrate the dark of the room and his ears listened for other sounds. He had been certain that the noise, what he explained was "sharp as a pistol shot," had come from the middle of his room.

Waiting for his eyes to adjust to the dim light, Watson slipped out from under the covers and took a few tentative steps toward the middle of the room. There he found something extremely odd. A large, heavy glass ashtray sitting atop a table in the middle of the room had cracked perfectly down the middle, leaving two equal sized chucks of thick glass.

Watson couldn't explain how the ashtray had seemingly instantaneously split in two in the middle of the night with nobody else in the room.

The following evening, another sudden loud noise in the dead of night awoke him. This time it was a crash in the washroom.

Again, when Watson managed to slip out from the bed and walk over to the bathroom to investigate, he found that his shaving kit (which he had most certainly secured behind the faucet earlier that evening before retiring to bed) was lying on the floor on the other side of the bathroom.

In a letter about the events that Watson wrote to author Joan Rankin, author of *Meet Me at the Château,* he explained how disturbed they left him. "Both of these events, trivial though they sound, were inexplicable and left me quite shaken. I will never forget them."

And whether or not you believe the apparently supernatural occurrences that have been experienced and reported at the Château Laurier, one thing can be certain: the building itself stands proud, majestic, and magnificent in a central part of the nation's capital, having stood witness to so many activities central not just to the forming of our capital city but to events that shaped both Canada and the world.

The ghosts and echoes in time from those elements alone are enough to regard the building with a significant degree of awe.

The Monster of Muskrat Lake

There is a monster, a cryptid creature that greets all those entering the small town of Cobden, Ontario. It appears on signs welcoming visitors on the highway and in front of the Home Hardware store. Never portrayed as fearsome, the creature, which allegedly lives in the nearby lake, has become a cultural mascot for the area and is even provided with seasonal accessories, such as a Santa Claus hat for Christmas, bunny ears for Easter, and sunglasses in the summer. And instead of fearing its proximity to the town, residents have embraced the tales of its existence.

About one hundred kilometres northwest of Ottawa, located in the Whitewater Region of Renfrew County and near the Ontario–Quebec border, lies a lake that is 16 kilometres long, 1.6 kilometres wide, and has a depth of between 18 and 60 metres. Like many lakes in Ontario, Muskrat Lake was formed ten thousand years ago when the glaciers of the last ice age began to recede.

The area around the lake was originally inhabited by one of the Algonquin tribes of the area. Samuel de Champlain was the first European explorer to reach the area, and he described the lake as "six leagues long and two wide, very abundant in fish."

Something Champlain did not note in his journals, however, was the existence of a creature that has come to be known as Mussie, which is short for "The Monster of Muskrat Lake." And had he encountered an aquatic creature like Mussie in the Ottawa Valley, he most certainly would have written about it, particularly since the explorer complained at length in his journals about the screaming of the sea monsters off the Grand Banks keeping him up at night.

According to local historian James F. Robinson, a creature has been reported in the lake since 1916 and is described as "having three eyes, three ears, one big fin halfway down its back, two legs, one big tooth in front, is silvery-green and stretches for twenty-four feet."

Originally named *Hapyxelor* or *Hapaxelor*, the creature's age, gender, and physical appearance varies in different accounts. At times is had been described as a three-eyed Loch Ness Monster, and legends are unclear as to whether these is a single creature of a species of "Mussie" living in the long and deep lake.

In the fall of 1988 Michael Bradley, author of the book *More Than a Myth: The Search for the Monster of Muskrat Lake*, and friend Deanna Theilmann-Beann set out to search for Mussie in a small custom boat (called *Nepenthe*) with sonar technology. On October 5, the sonar reading revealed what he interpreted to be two large creatures, at least three metres long, swimming toward the surface. Bradley concluded that at least one of them was likely the cryptid known as Mussie.

Bradley also interviewed a number of eyewitnesses from the area who had reported seeing the alleged creature. In sightings between 1968 and 1988, the creature's length was described as being anywhere from 2 to 3.5 metres long, possessing a rounded head, a long and thick rounded body, described as being "silver green" or "dusky red" in colour. Unlike the Loch Ness Monster, he didn't find any witnesses who claimed the creature had a long neck. One person who observed Mussie said that the creature appeared to have fins, and another person described a long tooth protruding out of its mouth. These descriptions led Bradley to consider that the creature might be some sort of aberrant species offshoot of a freshwater walrus or seal.

In his book, Bradley listed a number of possible explanations for the creature, including that it might have been oddly shaped rolling waves, which can often play tricks upon the eye, particularly in a certain light.

He also suggests that Mussie might be a relict species of plesiosaur, which is a warm-blooded dinosaur with a small head, long thin neck, a thick body, and flippers. This is the same type of creature that Nessie, the Loch Ness Monster, is often assumed to be.

A person regularly mentioned when the topic of Mussie comes up is a local businessman and fisherman by the name of Donnie Humphries, who is known to have seen the creature on multiple occasions. On some occasions, Donnie saw Mussie eating cattails along the shore; another time he spotted the creature's head popping out of the surface of the water.

Scientists and journalists continue to return to Cobden and Muskrat Lake to take sonar readings and write stories. And every summer tourists appear in order to try to find the monster.

"No one ever found anything," says Doug Schauer, owner of the Home Hardware store that has a cartoon version of Mussie welcoming visitors. "Which doesn't prove anything. Some of those holes on Muskrat Lake are just unimaginable, they are so deep."

Also deep are our beliefs that there are more things walking about on this planet than we can ever truly understand.

And so, the legends of Mussie in the Ottawa Valley, and Nessie in Scotland, continue to be shared from generation to generation.

The Lumber Merchant's Ghost Guide

Not all ghosts are frightening to behold.

Some, in fact, appear in a person's life at precisely the right time, in order to guide them to safety. They might be seen as types of guardian angels, there to look out for others, or perhaps to make sure that other people do not go down the wrong path like they might have done.

This article, from a January 1891 *Ottawa Citizen*, was written as a retrospective forty years after the lumber merchant had experienced it. The locale for the tale must have been just across the river from Ottawa and involves a mysterious stranger who appears out of nowhere to act as a guiding light.

My Ghostly Guide — A Lumber Merchant's Story

In January 1853 I was engaged as assistant clerk in a large lumbering camp in the woods about a hundred miles north of the Ottawa river. Our main shanty was by the side of an outlet of Red Pine Lake about two miles from the south side of the lake itself, a sheet of water of oblong shape, about a mile and a half wide and five miles long. There was a fairly good road from the edge of the lake to the shanty, and from the north or opposite side of the lake, a road had been made for some miles through the forest, to a point where a smaller camp had been established, and where a number of our men were engaged in making timber. From the main shanty to the smaller one was probably twenty miles.

One day my chief, Mr. Simpson, sent me off with some instructions to the foreman in charge of what we called the Crooked Creek camp. I started with my snowshoes on my back and moccasins on my feet, at a brisk pace.

It was a bright clear day. The road to the lake had been "well worn" by teams, and as there had been a thaw covered with frost, the ice on the lake was hard and smooth. The road from the lake to the Crooked Creek camp was rather rough and narrow, and a stranger might have difficulty in following it. However, I knew the route well, and arrived at my destination in good time, just as the men were returning from their work, with axes on their shoulders. I spent the night in the camp, being asked innumerable questions, and hearing all the petty gossip the men had to relate. It must be remembered that these shantymen go into the woods in October or November and excepting in rare instances hear nothing whatever from the outside world until they come out in the spring. Next morning I executed my commission and about ten o'clock started back for the main camp. I had not travelled more than half the distance when a snowstorm set in. In the woods the flakes fell down steadily, and I had no difficulty in keeping the road. It was about sun-down when I reached the edge of the lake. The snow had covered the track across the ice and there was nothing to guide me to the entrance to the road to our main camp on the opposite shore. Out on the lake the storm was blinding, but I did not doubt my ability' to reach the other side and find the road. So I started across the lake. When less than half a mile from the edge of the woods the snow was so thick that I could see neither shore. Moreover it was getting dark and exceedingly cold. If I should lose my way on the lake and have to spend the night there I would certainly perish. What was to be done?

I turned in my tracks and managed to reach the north shore again, stepping in the shelter of some bushes to recover my breath. Should I stay there all night? To tramp back to Crooked Lake camp was my first decision, but on reflection I remembered that any person travelling that road at night was liable to be attacked and eaten by wolves. Moreover I was hungry and fatigued.

While I was thus communing with myself, jumping up and down and slapping my hands to keep myself warm, I saw a man dressed in a grey suit with a toque on his head and a scarf around his waist, about 200 yards out on the lake, beckoning to me to follow him. I at once jumped to the conclusion that Mr. Limpson had sent one of the axe-men to meet me and guide me across the lake.

So I ran with all my might toward him, calling to him at the same time. When I came close to the spot where he had stood, I looked around. He was not there, but a lull in the drift showed him some distance further on, still beckoning me to follow. No reply came to my calls to the man to wait for me, but every few moments he would appear some distance ahead beckoning me toward him. I could not tell what to make of the man's eccentric behaviour, but thought possibly he was angry over being sent out to look me up, and was taking this method of evincing his displeasure. At last I saw him on the shore, pointing toward the woods, and reaching the spot where he had been standing I found myself at the point where the road to our camp left the lake. The road was easy to follow, and I hurried forward, still somewhat puzzled over the refusal of my guide to wait for me; and wondering also why he had not brought a horse and sled. I reached the camp just as the men had finished their supper, and everybody was surprised at my return. Mr. Simpson said he supposed that even if I had started from Crooked Creek camp in the morning I would have turned back when the snow storm came on. Somewhat bewildered I asked which of the men it was that guided me across the lake and pointed out the road to the camp, "Why did he not wait for me?" I asked in a rather injured tone.

The men looked at one another in amazement. Not a man had been out of the camp that evening. Every man had returned from work at the usual time and remained in camp until my arrival. We were nearly seventy miles from the nearest settlement and there was no camp nearer than the one at Crooked Creek. Every person in the camp became restless and nervous. That man who guided me across Red Pine lake was not a being of flesh and blood, was the general conclusion of the shanty-men and my description of his disappearances and reappearances tended to strengthen their theory. The experience was such an inexplicable one that very few of the inmates of our camp slept that night. I was grateful for my rescue, and it was evidently that whoever my guide was it was not my destiny to be eaten by wolves or frozen to death in attempting to cross Red Pine Lake in a snow storm.

Stomping and EMF Spikes at the Heritage Inn

Known as the "Grand Ole Lady" of Carleton Place, the heritage building at 7 Bridge Street has been home to much elegance and intrigue, as well as many tragedies that it seems to have only survived as if by some divine hand.

Perhaps the most well-known story involves an icon of Canadian music, Stompin' Tom Connors, who is credited with helping to spare the building from demolition back in 1990. But before we look at that, and at some of the eerie tales involving the building, let's take a quick journey through its history.

Napoleon Lavalee built the Mississippi Hotel from Beckwith limestone in 1872. It was used as a hotel as well as the location for town council meeting until at least 1883, and the twenty-eight-room inn was touted as one of the finest hotels between Ottawa and Toronto.

It has been said that there were three deaths in the hotel during Lavalee's ownership, although no official records have been found to confirm those stories.

Lavalee sold the hotel in 1883 to Walter Mcilquham, who increased the room capacity to fifty-six. The hotel stayed in the Mcilquham family until 1959. In April of that year the hotel suffered a devastating fire. The blaze, which lasted for five hours, completely destroyed the fourth floor.

A firefighter by the name of James Garland lost his life while heroically struggling against the flames.

On a warm day in early June a lanky and relatively unknown singer walked into the hotel carrying a guitar and a piece of plywood. The plywood, or "stompin' board," quickly became one of the legendary singer's trademarks. He allegedly carried it with him to stomp on so that his vigorous foot stomping would not damage the stage. Tom Connors introduced himself to the owner, Mrs. Lorraine Lemay, auditioned, and then began performing there on a regular basis.

In an interview, Lemay recalled how Connors had worked on the lines of "Big Joe Mufferaw," a song that would become one of his most well-known hits. "He kept asking me, 'Do you think it's any good Mrs. Lemay?'"

During the late 1970s the hotel fell into disrepair. In the early 1980s the hotel was purchased by Brian Carter and it became a biker bar, known for its sultry striptease shows. Further rumours surfaced of two deaths that took place in the hotel during this time. One was, allegedly, the death of a small boy who suffocated after being locked in a closet while his parents were enjoying a carnal tryst, and the other was of a female performer who hanged herself in one of the rooms.

In 1985, the seedy version of the hotel closed its doors and it sat abandoned for half a decade. By 1990, it was slated for demolition, but was saved by an upwelling of local support. A local musician by the name of Lyle Dillabough wrote to Stompin' Tom Connors, who by that time was mostly retired, asking for his support. While Connors refused all requests for live interviews, he released a written statement: "All that can be done must be done to preserve this 'Grand Ole Lady.'"

"So when he made that public statement the nation's media went into a bit of a frenzy." Dillabough said. "That had everything to do with why the Grand Ole Lady still stands at the corner of Bridge Street and Lake Avenue today."

The hotel went through a series of owners, but the state it was in was a mere shadow of the glory it had once possessed. Things began to turn around when Perry and Stephanie Seccaspima bought the property and began to restore it to its former glory, opening a bar and restaurant named Guido's, an homage to Perry's Italian-Canadian ancestry.

On July 18, 2014, the latest incarnation of the building began, with Lori and Larry Shepherd, who leased the building from the Seccaspimas, christening it the Carleton Heritage Boutique Hotel.

"The Carleton Heritage Boutique Hotel combines character, quality, service, comfort and value-added extras, making this boutique hotel the choice for residents and travellers lucky enough to be a part of Carleton Place, even if they are just passing through," Lori Shepherd said in a press release.

At the grand opening, Carleton Place Mayor Wendy Leblanc, who helped cut the ribbon, said, "This wonderful building has seen so many years of history in Carleton place. It's been an anchor for our historic town as the town hall is at the other end…. It's grown and thrived and not thrived, so it's wonderful to be here today to see it come back to life."

Of course, even when the hotel was vacant and stood empty and unused, there are those who believe that some of the many people who allegedly died in the building were still there.

Having heard the stories and eerie tales, members of C.H.A.P.S. (The Canadian Haunting and Paranormal Society), a science-based research group founded by Dave Gibb in 2006, conducted two different investigations in the building in January of 2009.

The crew consisted of several guests and three mediums. The names Heddy, Jacob, and Stan were all felt by the mediums, and members of the team felt heavy chests and reported what seemed like a smoke-filled hallway. There was thought that the smoke might be an echo from the fire that destroyed the top floor of the building in April 1959, but the team didn't find enough scientific evidence to support the claims of a haunting, and left with an undetermined verdict.

The team returned on March 16 to conduct a more thorough investigation. This time their devices picked up all manner of different phenomena. A video documenting their discoveries was uploaded to YouTube on March 24, 2009.

While wandering about one of the halls, Team One recorded an EMF (electromotive force) spike of 2.4 that immediately went down to a 0.6. The same thing happened on a couple of different occasions. It was almost as if the spirit was playing with the investigator.

EMF spikes of 1.3 appeared when the name "Mildred" was spoken in one of the suites. Then, shortly after, when the names "Mildred" and "Miley" were repeated, the spike went up to 5.4 before dropping back down to 0.5.

On other occasions, the EMF spikes went up to 3.9 then back down to 0.3 again. And the highest increase in EMF was when it shot up to a high 6.8.

Of the four CCTVs located in various rooms throughout the hotel, there was the occasional visible orb floating, as if toward the cameras, on a couple of them. Orbs, small circular artifacts, are thought to represent either spirits or energy captured on film. One of the other CCTV cameras was turned to a different direction when there was nobody in the room. The incident of the unseen hands moving the camera from facing the bed to facing the wall was caught on film.

EVPS (electronic vice phenomenon) captured what sounded like a male voice saying "real cool shadow," and at another point in the recording the word "Rockcliff."

Most intriguing is something that the team hadn't noticed until they were going back through their footage. There is video from a still cam of two of the investigators moving slowly through the dark in the ballroom, having a conversation. Behind them and to the right there is a very distinctive shadowy shape that appears to get up from a chair and walk out through a nearby exit.

The verdict, after this second investigation, was that the building was definitely haunted.

Regardless of whether you believe the stories and reports of ghostly occurrences in the building, one thing is for sure: standing in the same place that a legendary musician began his rise to fame, one can't help but hear the echoes of the past, presenting in the sound of a foot pounding eternally on a plywood board atop an invisible stage.

The Ghost That Sighed

Sometimes an event happens that is so startling and dramatic that it draws people from miles around. Reporters and spectators flock, unable to believe what they just heard or saw. And, occasionally, even the naysayers, or those who usually are able to find logical explanations for someone else's perceived spooks and ghosts (a phrase once used for this was to "layer" or to "lay" a ghost), come up empty handed, shrug their shoulders, and shake their heads.

Such is the case in this tale of some mystifying noises coming from an old farmhouse on the Rideau Canal near Merrickville in 1893. Below is the March 8, 1930, article from the *Ottawa Citizen*.

> **Story of the Mystifying Noise in a Farm House; Ghost That Sighed or Gasped And Moved About: Peculiar Happenings About Year 1893 On Rideau Canal Near Merrickville**
>
> *Odd Noise, as of Dying Man's Gasp Which Drew Hundreds of Farmers From All the Surrounding Countryside — Ottawa Newspaper Ghost Layers Were Baffled and Returned With a Striking Story.*

One of many memorial markers for the workers who died building the Rideau Canal. This Celtic Cross, located on the lower locks in Ottawa, reads: "In Memory of 1,000 workers & their families who died building this canal 1826–1832."

Author's collection.

This is the "Story of the Ghost That Sighed." The "thing" or series of "demonstrations," occurred about the year 1893, in a farm house about three miles south of Merrickville, on the bank of the Rideau canal. At the time the demonstrations were going on the editor of the Old Time Stuff was one of the "star" reporters on a city paper, and had secured some little reputation as a layer of ghosts and an exposer of charlatans of various sorts for his paper.

In the summer of 1893 there sifted to Ottawa stories of peculiar noises which were being heard in a farm house outside of Merrickville. It was said that the demonstrations were most mysterious and baffling, and that the whole countryside was flocking to the locale of the noises.

Sent to Scene.

The managing editor of the paper suggested that the writer should proceed to the scene and see if he could "lay" the ghost. The writer jumped at the opportunity, but stipulated that he should take with him another bright young man of the staff as co-investigator, and as things turned out his co-operation was much needed.

Sent on the Trail of the Mystifying Noise.

The young man who was selected as assistant for the job is now a prominent civil servant and head of a leading branch of the service.

The writer and the other bright young man set off Saturday morning for the scene of the "demonstrations" and arrived at Merrickville that night. The managing editor had thought it wise for the investigators to be on the scene on Sunday instead of a week-day, as it was on Sunday that the farmers from the surrounding townships gathered at the place. It had been hinted to the newspaper that that for some reason the "spook" operated best when there was a crowd around.

Was a Crowd.

So it happened that Sunday afternoon found the two investigators on the job at the scene. And one glance showed that the stories that had been told about the crowds that were going had not been exaggerated in the least. The house was surrounding be a heterogeneous collection of vehicles. The farm yard was full of buggies, carts, hay wagons, etc. The hay wagons had been used to bring parties of young people.

No Names Mentioned.

The Old Time Staff will not mention the name of the owner of the farm nor attempt to locate its whereabouts too closely, as the eerie reputation which the place then had may have long ago worn off and been forgotten.

Dramatic Scene.

The two reporters not having had any details as to the nature of the "spook" were a little surprised when they entered the house to find the large old-fashioned kitchen and the dining room full of very silent people sitting or standing in a tense silence and an expectant attitude. Not knowing what the thing was all about, the reporters walked into the kitchen without any particular quietude and were as a consequence greeted with hostile looks from about thirty people, and a sibilant "Hush!" from a man sitting hear the door.

Watchful Waiting.

Taking the hint, the reporters found their way on tiptoe into a corner and waited till they could get their bearings and the reasons for the "hush."

In the room a dead silence was prevailing. It was as though the occupants were either at a "wake" or in the presence of an awful tragedy of some sort.

The newspapermen began to wonder whether they had made a mistake and got into a house of mourning. After waiting for about five minutes in the kitchen and not hearing anything, the writer mentioned to his coadjutor to go outside and followed him.

Getting the Lowdown.

Once outside they proceeded to question one of a score or more of men who were standing around smoking. From this man they learned more or less what it was all about. It appeared that a couple of months before the owner of the farm, an old man, had died. Shortly after his death, peculiar noises began to be heard in the house. These noises were entirely different from the noises ordinarily heard in a haunted house. There were no knockings or rattling of chains or things of that sort.

Indefinite Noises.
On the contrary, the noises were so low and indefinite as to prevent one from being able to really describe them. The general opinion of the visitors seemed to be that the nearest description of the noise what that of a sigh or a sort of "u-u-g-h." Some had described it as the last gasp of a dying man and that suggestion seemed to find favor.

Re-entered.
Armed with the information, the reporters re-entered to hear what they could hear. They found in the kitchen seats that had been vacated (for the people were coming and going to relieve the tension) and sat down to listen.

The investigators, knowing what they were expected to hear, had decided to signal each other as soon as one or the other heard anything which sounded like a supernatural noise.

Noise Soon Came.
They had not long to wait. From somewhere in the kitchen there came a faint and almost indescribable noise, which might equally well be described as a gasp or a sigh. The noise had the slighted suggestion of a tremolo.

Not Heard Same Place.
One of the investigators indicated by a sign that he had heard something. The other nodded, indicating that he also had heard. The first investigator pointed to a certain part of the room as being the spot where he had heard the noise. The other shook his head and pointed to another spot.

Then they went out for a conference. When they went into the house again they tried the dining room. There also after a duration the noise was heard — low and elusive.

In Two Rooms.
And further enquiry developed the fact that when the noise was being heard in the kitchen it was not being heard in the living room. It was as though whatever was making the noise was going from room to room. It gave one an uncanny suggestion.

After another conference the investigators decided to try for themselves other parts of the house. They went upstairs. Nobody tried to stop them. There was nobody upstairs. It was evident that the family had given over the house to the country-side.

Only On One Floor.
Investigation proved there was no "noise" upstairs. Then the investigators tired the cellar. No noise there. The cellar had a natural stone floor with seams in it. It occurred to the reporters that as the house was only about a quarter mile from the Rideau river it might be an escape of air from a rock seam having an outlet to the river. But that theory was given up, as neither gasp nor sigh was heard in the cellar.

The parlor was next visited with negative results.

Watched the People.
Then the investigators began to watch the people who were sitting around, to endeavor to ascertain whether any of them were making the noise or noises. It could not be traced to any of them.

But the nose, whatever it was, was definitely located in the two rooms — the kitchen and the dining room. It was told to the reporters that the probably reason for that was the fact that the old man who had died had had his bed in the dining room when he passed away.

To get on with the story, it may be told that the investigators stayed in the house for over five hours but could not get any definite line on that noise, nor could they agree at any time just where the noise was. Sometimes it was low down, sometimes high up, sometimes in the center of the room, sometimes near a corner.

Baffling Noise.
It was the most baffling noise the investigators had ever heard — and always faint and indefinite.

And all the time the visitors were coming and going, waling silently in and silently out. And frequently came the warning "Hush!" as some newcomer made too much clatter.

Not Constant.
It should be explained that whatever the noise was, it was not constant. Far from it. There was often a 5 to 10 minute wait between demonstrations. Sometimes, on the contrary, there would only be two or three minutes.

No Place for Deaf.
And all the time the people, men and women girls and youths, were straining their ears. It was no place for a deaf person.

Evening came and the reporters began to think about the next day's paper and the story they had to write. They left the scene regretfully, confessing that they were going away no wiser, as to the cause of the sound, than when they came. The ghost-layers had been baffled.

A Great Story.

Anyway the thing made a great story when it was written. The O.T.S. does not know what the outcome of the thing was. It does not know whether the noises are still being heard or how long they lasted. If an explanation was found the O.T.S. will be pleased to hear what it was. Perhaps the Ottawa investigators might have found an explanation if they had had more time. But they didn't find one.

The Ghostly Violin

According to a story relayed to the *Ottawa Citizen* by Richard Lendrum of McLeod Street in a 1930 newspaper article, a stone home on the shores of the Ottawa River about four miles west of L'Orignal became haunted by the ghostly wailing of a violin.

In a mid 1840s dispute over payment for carpentry work in a newly built house on the bank of the river, a carpenter cursed the owner, claiming he would never have any luck with the house, and the house itself. The carpenter said that when he died he would come back and haunt the place.

"And it won't be very nice music you will get," the carpenter was said to have added.

The carpenter, you see, was a very fine violinist and regularly, during his breaks and in his spare hours, had played the violin while the house was being built.

A few years later, when the carpenter died, the curse he had set forth seemed to have come true. Strange things began to happen in the house and every night, as the hour neared midnight, the strains of a violin could be heard. The strains were not the normally beautiful haunting notes of a master violinist; they were of a weird discord and carrying sharp notes of anger.

Unable to bear the painfully agonizing noises in the middle of the night, the owner was forced to vacate the premises and the building sat vacant for many years.

Occasionally some tenants would move into the building, but none stayed very long. They were obviously disturbed by the ghostly violin sounds echoing through the dead of the night.

Sometime in the mid 1850s an older French man and his wife arriving from Prescott County acquired the empty house.

Despite the ongoing stories about the ghostly violin, the old man and his wife remained.

Curious neighbours arrived at the home around ten o'clock one evening and questioned the old couple about why they stayed despite the haunting and eerie violin sounds in the middle of the night. The two readily admitted that they could not afford to leave. They were poor, had invested all of their savings into acquiring the home, and were unable to make another move.

"And now," the old man told his visitors, "you had better go home. We must go to our beds. And anyway, that man will soon be here."

The visitors, morbidly curious about the stories they had heard, asked if they could remain after the old couple had retired to their bedroom.

"Very well," the old man said, shaking his head. "You will surely be sorry. You do not have to stay, but we do."

Nervously, the visitors laughed and admitted that they were anxious to hear the ghost that they had heard so much about.

"As you wish," the old man said. "But be sure to shut the door behind you when you go out."

After the old man and woman retired to their bedroom, the visitors sat nervously in the living room, looking at and watching the fire in the fireplace. Save for the occasional cracking of the fire, the night was quiet and the air still.

Then, suddenly, an apparition appeared in the guise of a young man with a violin braced under his chin. The visitors sat there, stunned, as they watched him walk across the floor. Without looking at them at all, the ghostly man walked straight to the stairs and ascended them.

Shortly after the spectre holding the violin disappeared upstairs, an ungodly wailing sound cascaded through the house. It was a screeching and angry cacophony of notes sliced into the air in a violent and ear-shattering manner. The terrifying wailing of the music was so powerful, so filled with an intense energy, that it was painful to listen to.

With their hands clasped over their ears, the visitors fled from the house, relieved to escape it once they passed back out through the front door.

In relaying the story, Mr. Lendrum did offer a bit of a happy ending, at least for the old French couple. Apparently, after a bit of time, they managed to put aside enough money to finally leave the horrific home.

It is not clear if anybody ever tried to move in there again.

The Controversial Carp UFO Case

A compact rural community of just under two thousand people, located about thirty kilometres northwest of Ottawa on the Carp River, is a quiet town named for the abundance of the freshwater fish that the river was once overrun with.

One of the more popular attractions in Carp is the decommissioned Canadian Forces Station Carp, a Canadian military facility commonly known as the Diefenbunker that was originally a top-secret underground bunker designed to house key members of the Canadian government in the event of a nuclear attack.

In 1958, Prime Minister John Diefenbaker authorized the creation of fifty "Emergency Government Headquarters" across Canada. The one closest to Ottawa would be the largest at over 100,000 square feet, with four storeys underground, requiring 32,000 tonnes of concrete and 5,000 tonnes of steel. Meant to accommodate as many as 565 people for up to one month without requiring additional supplies from outside, the structure included a broadcast studio for the Canadian Broadcasting Corporation and a vault to hold the gold reserves of the Bank of Canada, and was capable of withstanding a five-megaton nuclear explosion from just under two kilometres away.

Courtesy of Jonathon Simister.

The blast tunnel entrance at Canadian Forces Station Carp (also known as the Diefenbunker).

The facility was operated from 1959 until 1994 by the Government of Canada Department of National Defence. The site was decommissioned in 1994 and taken over by the local municipality. Due to overwhelming demand from the public, who displayed an intense curiosity about the facility, a group of local volunteers undertook the task of opening the bunker as a Cold War museum where people could take public tours.

The museum, run completely by volunteers, opened in 1998 as a not-for-profit museum and received upward of five thousand visitors in the first year. In 1999 the number of visitors doubled, and almost fifteen thousand people passed through the Diefenbunker in the year 2000. By 2008, the museum saw an average of about twenty-five thousand visitors, and in 2012 more than forty-five thousand people went through.

While this Cold War-era bunker serves as an ongoing attraction to both locals and tourists, there's another element that draws people to Carp — the alleged UFO landing that took place there in 1989.

One of the most controversial UFO cases in Canadian history, the Carp-Guardian story has been the subject of numerous newspaper articles, chapters of multiple books, dozens of UFO-tracking and reporting websites, and was featured on the American television program *Unsolved Mysteries*.

In late 1989 a group of UFO researchers and investigators in both the United States and Canada received packages in the mail from a mysterious stranger calling himself "Guardian." Each package contained several items, including a photocopied photograph of an alien standing in some greenery, and a document describing a UFO crash that had taken place on November 4, 1989.

Following is the text of that document.

Canadian and American Security Agencies are engaged in a conspiracy of silence, to withhold from the world the alien vessel seized in the swamps of Corkery Road, Carp, in 1989.

UFO sightings in the Ontario region had intensified in the 1980s, specifically around nuclear power generating stations. On Nov. 4, 1989 at 20:00 hrs Canadian Defense Dept. radars picked up a globe shaped object travelling at phenomenal speed over Carp, Ontario. The UFO abruptly stopped, and dropped like a stone.

Canadian and American Security Agencies were immediately notified of the landing. Monitoring satellites traced the movements of the aliens to a triangular area (see aerial map) off Almonte and Corkery Roads.

The ship had landed in deep swamp near Corkery Road. Two AH-64 Apaches and a UH-60 Blackhawk headed for the area the following night. The helicopters carried full weapon loads. They were part of a covert American unit that specialized in the recovery of alien craft.

Flying low over Ontario pine trees the Apache attack choppers soon spotted a glowing, blue, 20 meter in diameter sphere. As targeting lasers locked-on, both gun-ships unleashed their full weapon loads of 8 missiles each. All 16 were exploded in proximity bursts 10 metres downwind from the ship.

The missiles were carrying VEXXON, a deadly neuro-active gas which kills on contact. Exposed to air the gas breaks down quickly into inert components. Immediately after having completed their mission the gun-ships turned around, and headed back across the border.

Now the Blackhawk landed, as men exploded from its open doors. In seconds the six man strike team had entered the UFO through a 7 meter hatchless, oval portal. No resistance was encountered. At the controls, 3 dead crewman were found.

With the ship captured, the US Air force, Pentagon, and Office of Naval Intelligence were notified. Through the night a special team of technicians had shut-down and disassembled the sphere. Early the next morning Nov. 6, 1989 construction equipment and trucks were brought into the swamp. The UFO parts were transported to a secret facility in Kanata, Ontario.

As a cover story the locals were informed that a road was being built through the swamp. No smokescreen was needed for the military activity as Canadian forces regularly train in the Carp region. Officially nothing unusual was reported in the area. Although someone anonymously turned in a 35mm roll of film. It was received by the *National Research Council of Canada*, in Ottawa. The film contained several clear shots of an entity holding a light (see photo). At this time the photographer is still unidentified.

The humanoids were packed in ice and sent to an isolation chamber at the Univ. of Ottawa. CIA physiologists performed the autopsies.

The reptilian, fetus-headed beings, were listed as CLASS 1 NTE's (*Non Terrestrial Entities*). Like others recovered in previous operations, they were muscular, grey-white skinned, humanoids.

The ship was partially reassembled at the underground facility in Kanata. Unlike previous recoveries this one is pure military. Built as a "Starfighter" it is heavily armed and armored. In design no rivets, bolts, or welds were used in fastening, yet when reconstructed there are no seams. The UFO itself is made up of a *matrixed dielectric magnesium alloy*. It is driven by pulsed electromagnetic fields generated by a cold fusion reactor. All offensive capabilities utilize independently targeting electronic beam weapons. In the cargo hold were found ordnance racks containing fifty Soviet nuclear warheads. Their purpose was revealed by advanced tactical/combat computers located in the flight deck.

Threatened by recent East-West relations, and the revolutionary movements within itself, Red China is preparing for the final ideological war. The *aliens have agreed to defend China* from the free world's combined military and nuclear forces.

At this time China is arming the Middle East with their own nuclear arsenals, in order that they can successfully take on Israel. Unifying the Arabs under one Chinese command was simple, especially with Israel's recent "iron fist" attitude toward occupied territories.

The Soviet warheads found in the UFO were destined for Syria. CIA operatives in the Middle East have noticed huge movements of Chinese "technicians" and "advisors". China is also supplying the Arabs with bacteriological agents, Migs, Hind gunships, tanks, and missile launchers. The use of "Soviet" instead of "Chinese" nukes is part of a disinformation campaign to break up East-West relations after the annihilation of

Israel. The Warheads were hijacked from Soviet subs in the *Dragon's Triangle.*

A section of alien controlled Pacific once frequented by Russian subs. After losing some 900 high yield warheads and 13 vessels, commanders were ordered to steer clear of the area.

The most important alien-tech find were the 2 millimeter, spheroid, brain implants. Surgically inserted through the nasal orifice the individual can be fully monitored and controlled. The CIA and Canadian Govt have actively supported mind-slave experiments for years. Currently the Univ. of Ottawa is involved in ELF wave mind control programs. A continuation of the CIA psychological warfare project known as MKULTRA, started at the *Allen Memorial Institute* in Montreal.

Using ELF signals transmitted at the same wavelength the human brain uses, the researchers could subliminally control the test subject. The alien implants utilize the same principles except that the whole unit is sub miniaturized and contained in the brain. Fortunately the implants can be detected by magnetic resolution scanning technology. All individuals implanted by the aliens are classified as ZOMBIES.

The ZOMBIES have been programmed to help overthrow Mankind in the near future. When China finishes with Israel it will invade Europe. At the same time Chinese space based bacteriological weapons will be launched at the Arctic. The winds will carry the diseases into Russia and North America. In days 100's of millions will be dead, survivors will have to deal with Chinese, aliens, and the ZOMBIES.

The aliens want all out war so that human resistance would be minimal, when they invade. They tried this same tactic once before with Nazi Germany. Most of the scientific advances we have today came from German science which was based on alien technology. Had Hitler won the war, the earth would have become a concentration camp in order to depopulate the continents for the aliens.

Data aboard the sphere explained why the aliens are so comfortable on our world. They preceded man on the evolutionary scale by millions of years; created with the dinosaurs. Some 675 million years ago an interdimensional war destroyed most of their civilization, and forced them to leave the earth. Now they have chosen to reclaim what was once theirs.

The alien forces with their Chinese and Arab allies will attack within the next 5 years.

Waiting longer than that would make it impossible even for the aliens to reverse the ecological damage inflicted on the Earth by Man.

The paranoid and absurd nature of this document allowed people to easily dismiss and label it the product of a conspiracy theorist's overactive imagination. The report claimed that not only did a UFO crash, but alien bodies were recovered and relocated. Also relocated were pieces of the flying saucer wreckage that were sent to Kanata. The cumulation of the document was a conspiratorial rant about aliens conspiring with the Chinese to implant humans with devices that would turn them into zombie slaves. Despite that, curious to understand why someone would plan such an elaborate hoax, several investigators attempted to trace the documents back to their origin.

One of the people to receive a package was Tom Theofanous, a MUFON (Mutual UFO Network) field representative from Toronto. His belief was that the package constituted a hoax, and he connected with a colleague from the Ottawa area, Graham Lightfoot, who began locally investigating the matter.

Lightfoot was able to easily locate the apparent site of the crash as well as some people who claimed to be witnesses. One of the witnesses was a woman named Diane, who shared that on November 4, 1989, she saw a bright light flying over her house followed by helicopters with search lights that appeared to be scanning the area. A pair of other witnesses, not named, claimed to be frightened by an intense white light shining in through their bathroom window and reaching right down their hallway, yet a pair of local amateur stargazers who had been out that night could not recall anything odd having happened at all.

Lightfoot also investigated the field and swamp where the alleged incident took place, but was unable to find any evidence of a spaceship having crashed there nor any traces of any sort of massive recovery operation that would have been necessary in order to clean up and hide the crash as the anonymous documents suggested.

Other investigators from MUFON and CUFORN (Canadian UFO Research Network) visited the area, interviewed residents and the previously mentioned witnesses, but ended up leaving with the feeling that the case was most likely some sort of a hoax.

In October of 1991, Tom Theofanous and several other UFO researchers received more packages from "Guardian" that contained no return address but did come with an Ottawa postmark. The packages varied, but among them the following items were included:

1. Three playing cards — an ace, a king, and a joker — all with handwritten notes on them
2. A map of the alleged crash site
3. A VHS tape with the label "Guardian" and a fingerprint on it
4. A black and white photograph of a white-faced alien standing in a field of tall grass
5. Forged "redacted" documents supposedly from the Canadian Department of National Defence

The VHS tape contained a video, shot at night, which "Guardian" claimed was of an alien spacecraft sitting in a field. In part of the video bright lights that looked like road flares can be seen to the left of the object. The only sound to the video was the distinct sound of dogs barking in the background.

CUFORN debated what to do about the new material and decided, in light of the season that was upon them, to wait until the spring before returning to investigate.

In March of 1992, an American MUFON investigator describing himself as a former NASA mission specialist contacted CUFORN. The man, who claimed to receive one of the mysterious packages from "Guardian," introduced himself as Bob Oechsler and agreed to meet Tom Theofanous and Graham Lightfoot in Carleton in May of that year.

On Mother's Day in 1992, Oechsler and his son met with Lightfoot, Theofanous, and five other UFO investigators for breakfast before heading up to Oeshcler's motel room where they could compare the different VHS tapes they had received.

Theofanous was a little skeptical about Oechsler's claims that he was an expert in video analysis and was quoted in a *MUFON UFO Journal* article stating the man had a "great deal of difficulty" connecting the video equipment. He became a little more skeptical when, as the group set out on a convoy of vehicles to check out the area laid out in the map sent by "Guardian," Oechsler took the lead instead of following the local guide, Lightfoot.

"I thought at the time that was pretty odd," Theofanous said. "How did Oechsler, who supposedly had never been to Canada, let alone this area, know his way, using side roads and making the correct turns toward our destination?"

The group was driving down a small hill when Oechsler, who had asked the group to keep an eye on their compasses in order to detect magnetic anomalies, slammed on the brakes in his truck. He claimed that the two compasses that were in the bed of his truck (with his son, the truck's passenger, keeping an eye on them) indicated there was something amiss. Theofanous and the others, who had been holding their compasses in their hands, recalled that they had seen nothing out of the ordinary on their devices.

At that spot, they noticed signs reading "Do Not Enter" and "Defence Canada Killing Technology Area." There were car and other four-wheeled vehicle tracks near these signs, which were riddled with bullet holes, and the group suspected that this particular field might have been used for army "War Games," and could have been, due to the sound of a dog barking from a house at the top of a nearby hill, the location of the "Guardian" video shoot.

The group eventually continued on their search, reaching a spot where they had to park their vehicles and continue on foot. The rough terrain, the wet, swampy ground that was soaking their feet, and the raging mosquitoes made the trek difficult. With darkness looming, the groups split up, with Oechsler and his son continuing to look for the landing site, and the others turning around to head back. It took about twenty minutes for them to return to where their cars were parked and they left a note on Oechsler's windshield letting the two know they would be at a local restaurant, twenty minutes or so down the road.

Thirty minutes after the entire group arrived at the restaurant, Oechsler and his son arrived and announced that they had found the spot where the UFO had crashed. When questioned on how they could have possibly found and examined the spot, and returned to their cars in such a short time period, particularly as it was getting dark, Oechsler just smiled without answering.

Theofanous and his colleagues confronted Oechsler and asked him what he was trying to pull. In return, Oechsler asked what was wrong with trying to make a buck. Theofanous retorted by saying there was nothing wrong with making money so long as it didn't compromise their ethics.

"No matter what or how good the story is," Oechsler said, "fifty percent of the people will believe you, fifty percent won't. All you have to care about is the fifty percent that will."

At that point, Theofanous and his colleagues decided to back away from the investigation and observe how Oechsler and his son would behave.

The following day, during an interview with the woman named Diane, she talked about the incident in 1989, then shared a new experience she said she had had in August 1991. At about ten o'clock one night, the sound of dogs barking prompted her to look out her bedroom window. When she did she spotted flames or flares and lights coming from the field behind her house. Then she spotted a silver ship landing close to the flares that landed on three legs. She drew a picture of what she had seen. The image resembled one that had been drawn by "Guardian."

Lightfoot and Oechsler collaborated to investigate the area where the UFO had reportedly landed, in the field behind Diane's home. Although it had been nine months since the alleged landing (nine months that included an autumn and a cold and snowy winter), Oechsler claimed to have spotted marks on the ground that must have been made by an object landing. Lightfoot, who was employed by the Ontario Federation of Agriculture, remarked that the scratchings on the ground looked a good deal like the marks that skunks would make when digging for grubs. Oechsler then indicated a set of nearby bushes that were dried and shrivelled, stating that it was clearly the result of radiation from the spacecraft. Lightfoot replied that they were juniper bushes and that they always looked shrivelled after a cold winter.

Diane and her family began to talk about the helicopter activity that also happened near their home. Low-flying choppers, some coming close enough to the house to blow shingles off the roof, were spoken of a great deal. The household filed a complaint with the RCMP on February 10, 1993, arguing that these helicopters (suspected of being part of some government cover-up of the UFO crash) were flying well below the legal five-hundred-foot floor. An investigation was launched, but, despite video evidence provided by Diane and her family, it was ruled that there wasn't enough evidence for a successful prosecution.

Meanwhile, Bob Oechsler had already begun bringing the case not only to national attention, but to international intention. He crafted a case that was convincing enough to attract the attention of two American television shows: NBC's *Unsolved Mysteries* and *Sightings* on Fox, which both aired the story in 1993.

Oechsler was featured in both programs as a prominent UFO expert. Both he and Diane appeared on several other television and radio programs, seemingly basking in the fame this incident brought them. Oechsler also went on a UFO lecture circuit in Canada and the United States.

Graham Lightfoot, who had maintained an interest in this local event while staying away from the majority of the spotlight, eventually learned that Diane had a friend by the name of Bobby Charlebois who was a UFO buff. Charlebois was known to have gone by the code name of "Guardian."

After further investigation and worrying over the incidents and reports made by Oechsler and Diane, Lightfoot wrote a letter to Bob Kiviat, producer of the NBC television program *Unsolved Mysteries*.

Bob Kiviat, Producer
Cosgrove/Meurer Productions

Dear Bob,

No doubt you've heard from Oechsler that there has been another sighting at Labanek's ... on Feb 17th '93. It was Diane's mother who saw the event at 11:10 pm, very close to the house. She was so frightened that she didn't call to Diane and no one else saw it. She said the craft was right over the garden which means it was within 50 feet of the house. It hovered there for a short while and moved south over the swamp, in the direction that the 1989 "crash" light was seen. It came back beside the house and then moved off out of sight over the swamp. She described it as having a flashing light on top and lots of light all around it. She pulled the curtains from the window, but didn't wake anyone else in the house. The next day a white helicopter arrived and flew over the same course.

Oechsler may or may not have told you he is working with the RCMP in trying to get Guardian's (Bobby Charlesbois) fingerprints. He tells me he is trying to get the RCMP to charge Bobby with a minor charge of forging DND documents to scare him into an admission. This is contrary to Oechsler's stated intent to Bobby, of not disclosing Bobby's identity if he wished to remain anonymous.

I am trusting you to keep my comments to you in confidence from Oechsler as I will no doubt be working with him again on this case. I have no problem working with him at arms length, but his methods and rather chaotic behavior bothers me. He has told me that he wants to set up a 24-hours a day, two week watch at the Labanek's since he feels the sightings will re-occur in the near future. He has no funding for this operation and told me he will seek help from your company in this regard.

This may all be a good idea, but my feeling is that these things will run their course, with or without 24-hour surveillance. In fact I'd hazard a guess that the event is less likely to occur with surveillance.

I've heard through the grapevine that the "expert" on the Sightings show claims he doesn't know who Oechsler is, never met him. It seems Sightings showed the tape to this "expert" and he said he didn't know what it was. Also MUFON is distancing itself from Oechsler after their credibility suffered with the Gulf Breeze story. It seems Oechsler wants to speak at their annual meeting and they don't want him there.

Oechsler has a lot of background information and he certainly has a lot of contacts that are invaluable in doing research of this nature. He is persistent in looking for evidence, yet at the same time he often tries to build a case to fit his preconceived story line.

This bothers me.

We have talked about his ego and wanting credit for everything he learns. That's OK by me. In the Labanek case he used a lot of material that I got for him. The show implied that he found Labanek's place from the Guardian map.

He could have spent weeks looking for the location on his own.

But what bothers me the most is his tunnel vision, that only he can find the answers.

— Graham Lightfoot

Much debate and multiple viewpoints have been posted regarding the incident, with letters from Oechsler and various members of the UFO research community speaking out against the reports, citing them as a convoluted hoax. In the spring and summer of 1994, the *MUFON UFO Journal* ran a three-part series of articles entitled "Uncovering The Guardian Caper" that outlined, in elaborate detail, the events as reported by several MUFON members.

In September 1994, Oechsler passed around a letter than had, in turn, been posted on countless bulletin board systems.

THE OECHSLER RESIGNATION

As of September 1st 1994, I will be retiring from UFO research and investigations.

My tenure in UFO research has in some ways been very rewarding, especially the many close friendships that I've developed and enjoyed over the years. In many other ways the effects of my involvement have been quite debilitating, especially to my family.

I don't like what I've seen this phenomenon do to otherwise concerned rational people, including myself. The malicious libel, slander, distortion and unchecked fabrication that runs rampant in the UFO field is destructive and counterproductive. My belief is that UFOs are indeed real and that the management and spokespersons for ufology suffer greatly from egocentricity and self-importance when the evidence is clear that few really care much beyond the novelty. Therefore, I've decided to extricate myself from this eternal abyss and return to the family life that I've sorely neglected.

My final effort over the course of the summer will be dedicated to writing and publishing the truth of the matter regarding the guardian UFO Landing investigation in the Carp area of Ontario, Canada. My archives and research will be turned over to a private research institute where my work will continue. The institute is dedicated solely to unmitigated academic discourse and scientific research. The institute wishes to remain anonymous at this time.

After September 1st, I will not accept any orders for UFO materials which I have made available to assist in my research costs. For those of you who have maintained an interest in my research efforts, I thank you sincerely for your support and encouragement. It is because of you that I regret that this decision has become necessary.

My final opinion is that there is no mystery to the UFO phenomenon, the real mystery involves the sociology of how it affects and polarizes those drawn to it. This may be the best reason for government secrecy. There is a great need for comprehensive change in the attitude and management of the current organizational approach to UFO study if the subject matter is ever to receive and retain the attention of serious scientific professionals.

My final recommendation for those seriously interested in the potential scope and possible origins of the UFO Phenomenon is to read "Hyperspace" by Michio Kaku (1994 Oxford University Press, non-fiction).

Farewell all of my friends, colleagues and antagonists, good luck in all your endeavours.

Signed: Bob Oechsler / family man

In reaction to Oechsler's resignation letter, MUFON Ontario commented that this had been the first time a self-styled "professional full-time ufologist" had quit as the result of controversy. They also stated that "serious ufologists will not forget his unscrupulous actions and we too will be there in future to point out his reputation to newcomers."

There have been countless other UFO events reported in the Ottawa area over the years, including an unidentified object reported to have darted across the sky and then go crashing into the Ottawa River in July 2009, but none of them have stirred as much controversy, nor brought so many eyes from so far away to such a quiet little part of the great city of Ottawa, as the controversy surrounding the Carp UFO.

Teen Ghostbusters
of the Dirty Thirties

While it is fun to share a ghost story, it's also fun to share a story in which a locale is believed by many to be haunted, but the determination of an intrepid explorer, with an inquisitive eye and the ability to cut through the fear and dig deeper into the situation, got to the bottom of what led people to believe there was a haunting taking place.

It's also interesting when, almost by accident, a person, or pair of people, can stumble upon the answer to something that even the brave had previously shied away from.

Such is the case in this 1935 *Ottawa Citizen* article about a pair of youths who solved the mystery of a local haunted house.

People Were Puzzled About Haunted House
Till Youths Solved the Mystery.

Practically every district in the Ottawa Valley appears to have had its "haunted" house at one time or another. According to James Conlin of 501 Laurier avenue west, who hails from up Osgoode way, there was one such place near the village of Russell fifty years ago that had the good people of that district puzzled for a considerable length of time.

It was an old log building on a vacant fifty-acre farm, which had been built by one Harriston, a pioneer back in the late thirties or early forties. Stories were told about strange noises emanating from this old building late at night and some of the more timid ones in the community were afraid to pass the place after dark.

No one had dared venture within the place to investigate, until one night two young men from Russell village took shelter there from a blinding rainstorm. While they were there they heard noises which sounded like someone pounding on wood, and the noises came from the direction of the roof. Next morning they decided to investigate, and what they found was a loose board in the gable end of the house hitting against a rafter. And thus ended the spooky career of another "haunted" house.

Prime Ministerial Advice from Beyond the Grave

Sir John A. Macdonald, who was a Father of Confederation and the first prime minister of Canada, was born in Scotland in January of 1815. His political career spanned almost a full half century, and he served as leader of Canada for nineteen years. The only prime minister to serve a longer term than Macdonald was William Lyon Mackenzie King, who served just two years longer.

Unlike Macdonald's American counterpart, George Washington, there are no cities named after the man, nor are there any massive monuments for Canadians to pay homage to. In 2001, Parliament declared January 11 Sir John A. Macdonald Day, but unlike days like Victoria Day it is not a national holiday and so mostly passes unacknowledged each year. Both the Ottawa airport and Ontario Highway 401 are named after Macdonald and George Etienne Cartier, a fellow Father of Confederation. Respectively they are the Macdonald-Cartier International Airport (named in 1993) and the Macdonald-Cartier Freeway (named in 1968); but rarely are either of those ever referred to by their "newer" names.

Interestingly, Mackenzie King became notable for conducting séances and communing with the dead, but few know that Macdonald was also known to dabble in the area. Much like many of the tributes to and accomplishments of Canada's first prime minister, which seem to go unmarked or uncelebrated, the following eerie tale is also little-known.

Sir John Sparrow David Thompson, who was to become Canada's fourth prime minister, was the last minister to see Macdonald before his devastating stroke in May 1891, which partially paralyzed him and led to his death on June 6, 1891.

Could this event have led to a connection between the two beyond the grave?

This article, reprinted from the Toronto newspaper *The Daily Mail and Empire* on December 4, 1897, is attributed to a woman by the name of Faith Felton.

Anecdote of Sir John Thomson
Curious Experience Related by Faith Felton
How the Conservative Premiere Was Interviewed By a Young Man Who Brought Spiritualistic Messages from Sir John A. Macdonald.

Sir John Thompson was never given to much speaking. He lacked the small coin of gossip and light badinage in a marked degree. His words were few and thoughtful. His attitude was that of the onlooker rather than the participant. Yet when time for speech arrived he was always ready.

This was noticeable in the House. When one of those breezes of disagreement so common in parliamentary debate sprang up between member and member, or party and party, Sir John — who usually sat in that atmosphere of absolute quietism which seemed in itself a strength to his followers — waited until the matter had gone far enough or threatened the dignity of the House, then he arose and spoke the few wise, judicial words that made instantly for peace.

In debate it was the same. His was always the final utterance upon any subject; not because of his official position, but because his few words summed up the entire matter. He was judicial always, and his impartial attitude won recognition and favour upon both sides of the House.

In private life he was much the same, speaking little but always a kindly observer; and nothing was more attractive to those privileged to meet him socially than his attitude of readiness to be interested and pleased. "I know I am not a talker; but I am pleased to hear you talk, and ready to listen," his quiet look and bearing said to all who approached him. And because of these abiding qualities of strong sympathy, and a thoughtfulness that was not secretive, wrapped in an atmosphere of quietism, Sir John was a prince of listeners.

Yet he enjoyed fun, as most quiet people do, and when in the privacy of a friendly circle the merry talk went round, he — the usually silent listener — would frequently arouse himself to contribute something — an opinion, may hap, or an incident out of high official experience — that was well worth the hearing.

It was on such an occasion, and only a few months before his death, that he related in the presence of the writer one of those curious experiences that, doubtless, occur to all men of high official position, who become naturally a mark for cranks and faddists.

That it relates very closely to the Old Chieftain, and has hitherto been known only to some three or four of Sir John's associates, will render it of interest to Canadians everywhere:

It was an August afternoon that last summer of Sir John Thompson's life, and in the company of his family and two or three friends he sat on the deck of a certain pretty yacht as it rippled its way across the waters of Lake Rosseau. The Premier had been silent, as was his wont, lying back in his chair with closed eyes, with only an occasional smile, showing that he heard the conversation carried on about him.

Presently the talk turned on hypnotism. Sir Mackenzie Bowell, who was an adept at the art in his young days, related certain stirring experiences of his personal explorations into the misty land of psychology; and urged on by the joking skepticism of Senator Sandford, offered to give practical illustration of his power on the spot.

Sir John roused suddenly into a decisive veto against the half-jesting proposal.

"The thing is all nonsense, of course, but we mustn't have anyone tampered with," he said; and as the conversation drifted on naturally to the subject of clairvoyance and dreams, he related the following incident:

I had been premier something less than a year, and Sir John Macdonald had been dead, as you will remember, a year or so, when one morning my private secretary came into my office and said that a young man wanted to see me, but would give neither his name nor his business.

As on enquiry he appeared to be respectable and well-mannered, I gave orders that he should be admitted.

On finding himself alone with me, he told me frankly that he was afraid I would be surprised at his errand.

"What do you want?" I said.

"I have a message for you from Sir John Macdonald," he answered.

I looked him over keenly; but he was evidently in earnest, and moreover seemed conscious of his position.

I enquired quietly what the message was, and in what manner he received it.

Sir John Macdonald had appeared to him distinctly on several recent occasions, he said, urging him to bring a certain message directly to me; and so strong was the influence exerted, that he felt impelled to relieve himself of responsibility in the matter of complying with what he believed to be a request from a departed spirit.

The message related to certain private funds that belonged to Miss Mary Macdonald, and which her father — so the young man asserted — desired to be transferred and otherwise invested.

After the young man departed I made a few enquiries concerning him. He came from Nova Scotia, and was engaged in temporary work at Ottawa in the Buildings. He belonged to a thoroughly respectable family, and up to the present bore no reputation for erraticism of any kind.

I mentioned the matter to the lawyer entrusted with the Earnscliffe investments, and he confessed himself at a loss to understand how the private affairs involved in the "message" could have come to the young man's knowledge since they were known only to himself. But he admitted that the course indicated concerning the funds in question might be sound business advice.

The matter had almost passed from my memory, when one day, several months later, the young man presented himself again with a second "message" from the same source, this time for myself. Sir John Macdonald was earnestly desirous that certainly changes should be made in the Cabinet.

I took the young fellow in hand and questioned him closely. As far as I could discover he was honest, and apparently an unwilling bearer of these peremptory messages.

Why they were given to him, he said, he did not know; but after they were given he had no peace with the nightly appearance of Sir John Macdonald reiterating his commands until they were filled.

Sir John Thompson's quiet face broke into a smile of amused remembrance at this point in his story.

"You would need to understand Sir John's well-known penchant for planning Cabinet changes," he said, "in order to appreciate the effect of this last 'message' upon my colleagues, whom I took into confidence in the matter."

They listened in silence; but it was Sir Adolphe Caron who voiced their thought in one expressive sentence:

"Good Lord!" he exclaimed, "is the old man at it again?"

"What were the proposed changes, Sir John?" queried one of his listeners when the laugh subsided.

"Ah, that is another story," he said, smiling. "But again the curious fact is that they were excellent suggestions, and just such changes as I should like to have made myself had it been practicable. Yet this young man knew nothing of politics — much less of the inner workings of the Cabinet."

The Faceless Ghosts of Richardson Side Road

Tales of ghosts appearing at the side of lonely stretches of highway are not at all uncommon; after all, isn't one of the most eerie things to imagine seeing somebody standing alone in the dark on the side of the road in the middle of nowhere? But the roadside ghostly tales typically involve a hitchhiking stranger who gets into the car and either says nothing or behaves in some strange manner before disappearing. It is as spooky as it is sad that this ghostly presence by the side of the road might never arrive at their intended destination but are, instead, doomed to continue to hitchhike for the rest of eternity.

In this particular tale, which takes place on Richardson Side Road in Carp, about thirty-five kilometres from downtown Ottawa, a few witnesses reported a figure on the side of the road behaving in a decidedly different manner.

One dark evening, a man and woman were driving with their son from nearby Kanata. Heading down a steep hill on Richardson Side Road in Carp, they were startled by something that suddenly lunged from the side of the road in front of their vehicle.

The woman, sitting in the passenger seat, screamed in terror.

But it wasn't just because she was startled at the sight of something darting into the road in front of them; it was because of what she saw.

The figure that quickly appeared was that of what the woman described as either a teenager or a young man wearing a baseball cap and several layers of clothing. Only the young man had no facial features whatsoever. And, instead of bouncing off the front of the passenger side of the car, the vehicle passed right through him.

The woman said that his face cast an unmistakably eerie white glow as it passed right by her on their way through the apparition.

Shaken, startled, and not understanding what was going on, the woman looked in the rearview mirror and could see that the young man hadn't vanished but was still standing in the road. Another car was bearing down on him.

"Stop the car!" she told her husband, explaining that she wanted to hail down the car behind them and ask if they'd seen the faceless young man as well. Her husband, however, shaken by what he had seen, kept driving, hoping to put as much distance between the frighteningly faceless ghost and his family as possible.

Upon reading about this incident on the Toronto and Ontario Ghosts and Hauntings Research Society website, another user was curious to read the tale and related their own experience on that very same roadway.

They had been with a friend, driving home at about one o'clock in the morning when they spotted a young man with a baseball cap walking along the side of the road. As they got near, they could see two distinguishing features: the boy had no face and seemed to be almost glowing in the darkness.

He didn't lunge out into the road, but rather kept walking forward on some sort of nocturnal quest.

The two friends kept driving and hadn't thought much about it until they read the first lady's report that sounded suspiciously like the young man they had witnessed.

Who is that young man, and where could he have come from?

What might he be seeking?

The woman from the passenger seat who was nearest the faceless young man as the car drove straight through him admitted that neither her husband nor herself had shared the story with anybody other than family members, for fear of being ridiculed. And the main reason that she anonymously shared the story online was because of something else that happened around the same place.

At a later date, the woman had been driving along that same stretch of road during the day with her son in the car. They both noticed, at the side of the road and not far from where they had seen the faceless apparition, a white wooden cross sticking out of the dirt in the ditch. The woman pulled over and they got out to look at the cross. Apparently, it was to mark the spot where a young man had lost control of his truck and crashed into some nearby trees.

Could the faceless young man at the side of the road be the spirit of the young man who had died so tragically in that accident?

Could his spirit be wandering at the side of the road in an attempt to get home? Perhaps, when he jumped out in front of the car, he had merely been trying to hail down a ride, to get to whatever destination he had been headed for.

These are all good questions. But there's another question that burns even stronger: why does the man have no face?

There is a Japanese legend of faceless ghosts known as *noppera-bō*, which are known primarily for frightening humans. At first they appear as ordinary human beings, then their faces disappear, leaving a blank and smooth sheet of skin.

One of the most popular stories about the *noppera-bō* involves a man travelling along the Akaska road to Edo who came upon a young woman in a remote location whose cries he could hear as he approached. The man reached out in an attempt to try to console the woman, but when she turned to him he saw that she had no face. Terrified, the man ran down the road away from her until he came upon a vendor on the side of the road. He relayed the story to the man, only to be shocked as the man, after wiping a hand across his face, transformed into a *noppera-bō* himself.

These Japanese entities are more akin to demons appearing and impersonating humans than spirits trapped on the earth.

The Paranormal Guide website explains that faceless ghosts are believed to be entities or spirits that are unaware of their own identity. Perhaps through trauma or the unspeakable manner by which they passed from this earth, all memory of who they were is completely erased.

That does seem to be a possible explanation for the young man in the baseball cap spotted by multiple witnesses on the side of the road. Perhaps he is a lost soul, unaware of the tragedy that brought him to that locale, forever wandering along the road, unsuccessfully attempting to flag down vehicles for help, trapped in not knowing who he is or was.

The Relief of a
Steamer Ghost

It is a tradition that the captain will go down with his or her ship.

Given the ship captain's willingness to stick with their vessel even in the midst of a crisis, it is not a far stretch to imagine the spirit of that captain to remain steadfast to its appointed post in life.

Considering the commitment involved, it might not only be wise, but necessary, to perform some ritualistic procedure in order to exorcise the poor spirit from its otherworldly duties.

Like when a haunted boat was finally cleansed of its haunting spirits with a ritual blessing in this 1926 newspaper story from the *Ottawa Citizen*.

Sailors Claimed Boat Was Haunted
Priest at Ste. Anne Blessed It, and Noises Ceased.

In the year 1870 there piled on the Ottawa a steamer called the *Relief*. It was part of the Auger fleet of Montreal. The *Relief* drew barges of lumber shipped from the H.T. Bronson mills here to Burlington. In that year the *Relief* while in a storm on the St. Lawrence below Montreal upset and the captains were drowned, while the balance of the crew had a narrow escape.

In due time the *Relief* was got going again. But it was not long before the crew began to allege that they heard queer noises on the boat — knockings on the outside of hull, rappings on the boiler, also queer noises as of people walking on the decks.

Alleged Haunting.

It became believed by the crew that the boat was haunted. One night while the boat was laid up at St. Anne de Believue, the crew were prepared to leave in a body. A man named Lefebvre, who was a second pilot, suggested to the men that instead of leaving they should get the priest at the village to come to the boat and bless it and then the spirits would depart — if there were any, which Lefebvre did not believe.

Boat Was Blessed.

His advice was taken. The priest told his men they were foolish, but consented to bless the boat, which he did with due ceremony. Captain Wm. Bothwell, who tells the story (which he heard from Lefebvre) says that from the time the priest blessed the boat the noises were not again heard.

This story is on par with the story of how two church elders of Hull township in the sixties prayed for the departure of evil spirits from an alleged haunted house back in the Mountain road. In that case also the spirits were not again heard from.

The Murder of
Thomas D'Arcy McGee

The tragic story of Thomas D'Arcy McGee involves a first, a last, and a controversy. For Canadians McGee's assassination had as much emotional impact as the murder of Abraham Lincoln, just a few years earlier, had for Americans.

The only assassination of a Canadian federal MP happened early in Canada's history (the country was a mere nine months old) and to one of Canada's Fathers of Confederation. The man accused, tried, and convicted of McGee's murder, Patrick Whelan, was the last person to be publically hanged in Canada.

A popular pub in downtown Ottawa, D'Arcy McGee's, is where folks have gathered regularly at dusk for over twenty years in order to go on the historic and magnificent Haunted Walk of Ottawa tour.

Given D'Arcy McGee's role at the centre of a notorious assassination that culminates in a ghost story (outlined in detail in the following chapter about the Nicholas Street Hostel, which was a former jail), it is perfectly fitting for many of the ghost walks to begin there; it is almost as if it is some sort of homage to the original historic incidents.

Born in April 1825, Thomas D'Arcy Etienne Hughes McGee was born in Carlingford, Ireland. His mother, who was the daughter of a bookseller, taught him the history of Ireland at an early age. This knowledge was something he would later use in both his writing and political activities. He left Ireland in 1840, bound for North America and the United States. He emigrated from the U.S. to Canada in 1857. D'Arcy McGee was a poet and also worked on multiple Canadian and American newspapers; his writing often reflected his homeland as well as his views on defending the Irish Catholic right to representation in the assembly. He later became the minister of agriculture, immigration and statistics in the Conservative government that formed in 1863.

Initially a strong proponent for Irish freedom, D'Arcy McGee eventually became an advocate for Canadian Confederation and publicly denounced the Fenian Brotherhood, who were dedicated to freeing Ireland from British rule. The Fenians, who were largely made up of Civil War veterans from the U.S., aimed to conquer Canada and then trade it back to Britain for Irish freedom. McGee's political shift made the Fenians see him as a traitor to their cause.

On April 7, 1868, after participating in a parliamentary debate that went on well into the night, D'Arcy McGee was walking home down the dark and quiet streets from the House of Commons at approximately 2:00 a.m. He arrived at his boarding house at 142 Sparks Street and was knocking on the door for his landlady, Mrs. Trotter, to let him in when an unidentified assassin snuck up behind and shot him, at point-blank range, in the back of the head. The gun was said to have singed his hair.

Mrs. Trotter has just pushed the door open when she saw the flash of the gunshot and smelled the gunpowder. Thinking it was a firecracker and perhaps pranksters on the street, she pulled the door shut immediately.

She went on to say that she opened the door again a moment later and saw what she thought was a man learning up against the right-hand side of the door. "He looked like a man who had had a stroke," she said, "and was leaning against the wall to recover himself."

Mrs. Trotter then closed the door and went to retrieve a light. Returning, she noticed blood in the hall. Opening the door she saw the same man leaning over a little more stooped than before.

"The figure then fell back on the sidewalk straight from the door," she said. At that point that she recognized her border.

Later that same day, while fighting back tears, a visibly shaken John A. Macdonald reported the murder to the House of Commons, referring to D'Arcy McGee as "a hero who died a martyr to the cause of his country, whose hand was open to everyone, whose heart was made for friends and whose enmities were written in water."

D'Arcy McGee was given a state funeral in Ottawa and interred in a crypt in Montreal. His funeral procession in Montreal drew an unprecedented crowd of 80,000 from a city of approximately 100,000 people.

The man's death caused an uproar and public outcry that led to a significant amount of additional pressure on local law enforcement to find, arrest, and properly punish the assassin. Patrick Whelan, a local Fenian sympathizer, was accused, tried, and convicted, despite there not being any solid evidence to connect him to the crime. Whelan was executed by public hanging on February 11, 1869, with an audience of over 5,000 people attending.

There was, and continues to be, speculation on whether or not Whelan was actually guilty of D'Arcy McGee's murder or if he was a convenient scapegoat. This following article from *The Times* in 1876, less than ten years after Whelan's execution, is but one of many articles that shed light on the fact that the hasty conclusions regarding Whelan's guilt might have led to the wrong person being tried and executed for D'Arcy McGee's murder.

D'Arcy McGee's Murderer.
REPORTED CONFESSION OF A CRIMINAL.
It Turns out a Mare's Nest.

MONTREAL, May 31 — it is currently reported that a young man named Trotter, now under sentence of death for murder in New York, has confessed to having shot and killed Thomas D'Arcy McGee. From information received to-day from a resident of Ottawa, it appears that it was in Trotter's mother's house that McGee was lodging and was about to enter at the time he came to his death. Trotter was at the time (1868) a young of sixteen, and was a page in the House of Commons. He was the first to find the deceased lying on the foot path after the murder and to give the alarm. It is said the door of the house must have been fastened inside when McGee tried to open it, and it is supposed that this was done by the murderers to detain him until they would carry their diabolical purpose into effect. There are many other collateral circumstances connected with the murder which confirms the report now current, and it is hoped some steps will be taken before he treads the gallows to enquire further into the matter. Trotter was a witness at the trial against Whelan.

TORONTO, June 1 — In reference to the alleged confession of a man named Trotter, now lying under sentence of death in New York, regarding the murder of Mr. Darcy McGee, a Mr. Trotter, son of Mrs. Trotter of the Marlborough House here says he it was who gave evidence against Whelan at the trail and was a page at the time in the House of Commons, he believes the story has originated through personal spite, and intends to try to discover the originators of it, and if successful prosecute him.

The controversy surrounding Thomas D'Arcy McGee's murder and the trials that followed are not the only thing that people argued over, wrote about, and speculated on. And apart from the regularly presented "death hand" of D'Arcy McGee, which is a bit of a morbid thing to have on display in so many places, civilized people have long been fascinated with accoutrements involving death. Odd collectors of haunted and morbid artifacts have long been with us, such as this article from a 1892 *The Quebec Saturday Budget*, which covers the story of a door plate alleged to be the one from McGee's front door, complete with a bullet hole. Like the arguments surrounding the trial of his murderer, this historic article reveals the bile with which journalists can mock and belittle one another in their reporting.

A LITTLE TOO PREVIOUS.

The correspondent of a Montreal paper has been the fortunate discoverer of a very remarkable historical relic in some old curiosity shop in Quebec, being no other than the door plate of the late Thomas D'Arcy McGee. This door plate is made trebly interesting in that it bears unmistakably visible the dent of the pistol bullet by which the great man lost his life, the bullet having stuck the door plate after having passed through the body of the murdered man. This curious fact is, we think, a new contribution to the history of the event, and is the more remarkable when it is considered that the door plate was in Montreal, while the murder took place in Ottawa. The discovery is made known through the *Gazette*, with which the discovered is connected as correspondent. — *Montreal Witness.*

When D'Arcy McGee was shot he was living at Mrs. Trotter's boarding house, Ottawa, and it does not seem probable that his door plate would be on the door of a house which he did not own or rent. His residence was in Montreal, and he only went up to Ottawa to attend the sessions of Parliament. Mrs. Trotter's name and not Mr. McGee's would very likely be on the door of her house. — *Quebec Chronicle.*

Newspapers pretending to be smart ought to make sure of their facts before they speak. The editors of both these papers quoted are supposed to know something of the history of our country, but it is quite apparent that what they do not know on the subject would fill a very large volume. In the first place it was the *Telegraph*, not the *Gazette*, which unearthed this interesting relic. In the second place the *Witness* is wrong in stating that the door plate was in Montreal while the murder took place in Ottawa. In the third place the *Chronicle* is wrong in saying that the door plate of the house on the steps of which poor McGee was murdered bore the name of Mrs. Trotter, the lady who kept the boarding house, and not that of D'Arcy McGee. We were wrong ourselves in one particular, for the dent in the door plate was not, it appears, caused by the bullet of the assassin. In every other particular we were correct. A gentleman who has investigated the matter thoroughly makes the following report:

"There was, after the murder, a brass plate put up by sympathizing friends on the wall adjoining the entrance door where Mr. McGee boarded. This plate had no 'dint of a bullet' on its smooth surface, unless it has been made a target of since the memorable event; but that it existed and was removed and doubtless taken to Quebec by some loving friend after the destruction by fire of the Desbarats block, there is no reason to doubt. Quebec had been the scene of Mr. McGee's early public career in Canada, and his family home even when the scene of his labors was at the Federal Capital, and thus it was not fitting that the door-plate should be exhibited in the Ancient Capital; but the point is that the historical memento, marking the fatal spot and the date of the sad event, had been erected after and not before the death of the lamented statesman. Therefore, although the polished surface may have been considerably damaged, being removed after the destruction of the building, the scars it may bear are not those of the assassin's bullet."

And, while the debate and theories continue to roll on, Thomas D'Arcy McGee's assassination remains a chilling and disturbing reminder of the evil that men can do to one another. This particular tale doesn't have a ghost; at least not one that has any sort of restless spirit associated with D'Arcy McGee. There are, however, many stories about the accused and convicted assassin, Patrick Whelan, whose restless spirit allegedly haunts the old Ottawa jail.

Hamilton lawyer Dermot P. Nolan, who is writing a play about Thomas D'Arcy McGee, wrote in an April 2015 article in the *Hamilton Spectator* that the story of McGee's life is an astonishing piece of Canadian history and "the anniversary of his death is a reminder of the importance of celebrating the rich and too often forgotten history which made Canada, as it approaches its sesquicentennial in 2017."

In the days of Thomas D'Arcy McGee, it was common to make a plaster cast of a famous dead person's face that could be used for displays, so that people could remember the likeness of the deceased.

This was especially popular if no painting of the person existed. And, in 1868, photography was still very new and was not yet as common as it would soon be.

There was an issue, however, with making a plaster cast of D'Arcy McGee's likeness. Because he had been shot in the back of the head, with the exit wound likely destroying his face beyond repair or recognition, the facial damage was probably too extreme.

So, as a way to commemorate his oratorical skills —McGee was said to animatedly gesture with his hands while he made speeches — a plaster cast was made of his hand.

The original cast appears in Ottawa's Bytown Museum, along with several other mementos surrounding the murder and trial of Patrick Whelan, and copies of the cast appear in other locales, such as the pub named after this Father of Confederation.

Ghosts of the Old Carleton County Jail

If ever there was a way to describe hell on earth, it might very likely involve hundreds of tortured souls wailing, cursed to forever relive conditions that would be too unbearable for the toughest of animals, in filth, infestation, human waste, and disease. Women, men, and children crammed into spaces one wouldn't even consider keeping an animal in, all weeping uncontrollably or screaming out in pain and misery at all hours of the day and night. People being dragged by their hair to a torturous solitary confinement where leaping to one's death in a desperate attempt to escape the hellish conditions was a viable option.

This might sound like one of the fantastical paintings of hell by Hieronymous Bosch, but it was just one of many intolerable days at the Carleton County Jail.

The Carleton County Jail was not a place that anyone would ever want to be. Ironically, the very same building, now run as the Ottawa Jail Hostel, is a popular destination and among one of the cheapest places for overnight accommodations in the city of Ottawa.

When the jail, which was operated from 1862 to 1972, was finally closed, Hostelling International purchased the building and opened the hostel one year later, leaving much of the original structure intact in order to allow guests a unique experience of spending a night in "jail."

The website for the HI-Ottawa Jail Hostel has a banner that reads: "We bet you never slept in jail!" and boasts that there is no other accommodation like this in North America. The hostel even houses Canada's only jail bar, called Mugshots, which was rated by CBC Radio as one of the best underground music performance venues in the city.

But those who stay at the hostel might just be getting a far deeper, and far darker experience than just the novelty of sleeping in an old converted jail cell.

In March of 2015, my partner Liz and I, as part of a week spent in Ottawa conducting research for this book, took multiple historic tours in the city, including the "Ghost and the Gallows" in-depth tour of the jail. Our guide walked us up the stairwells and through several floors, checking out the cells, the gallows, death row, and listening to dozens of stories of both the history and some of the more disturbing activities that took place there over the years.

Liz and I often darted away or hung back for a few extra minutes to take pictures and examine in more detail some of the cells and creepy corners of the prison. We were trying to get a good sense of what it might be like to be alone in such an eerie place.

At one point Liz, ever the intrepid explorer who often lingered a bit longer at a particular station, was still on one of the floors while the rest of the group had proceeded up the stairs. I remained alone in the stairway, waiting for her and taking pictures. This was shortly after hearing our guide talk about some of the prisoners who, rather than face the horrors of life in the medieval-like jail, would jump to their death in the stairwell. The guide also shared the tale of a pair of inmates, sometime around the year 1910, who overpowered a prison guard and threw him over the railing to his death in that very stairwell.

For me, that stairwell, as I looked down at the grates that covered the space between the stairs to prevent such suicides and murderous acts, was one of the more ominous locales in the building. Something dark stirred in my heart when I was standing there.

A look down the stairwell from the top. Tour guides inform visitors that the metal barriers were installed to help prevent suicide attempts.

Author's collection.

Throughout the tour, our patient guide joked about the two of us being the stragglers in the group. But there was so much to take in, and there were intriguing factoids printed on many of the walls, that we were trying so hard to fully and properly absorb.

One thing I know is that, in the manner that I have gone on multiple ghost walks in Ottawa, I will need to return on another tour of the jail.

Liz is fascinated with the thought of staying overnight there the next time we visited the city, but she hasn't yet been able to talk me into it, mostly because of the multitude of unexplainable eerie encounters that visitors have had over the years. (I'll never claim to be anything but an easily terrified person who still jumps at odd creaks in the night and leaps into bed for fear of the monster under there who might just reach out and grab at my ankles.)

†

Older than Canada itself, the Ottawa Jail Hostel on Nicholas Street in Ottawa is considered one of the most haunted buildings in Canada and North America and is listed in a Lonely Planet top-ten list of the world's spookiest buildings.

In the first episode of the television program *Creepy Canada*, Terry Boyle, the show's host and the author of such books as *Haunted Ontario* and *Hidden Ontario*, described the building as being littered with spirits.

Located at 75-77 Nicholas Street, in between Wilbroad Road and Laurier Avenue East, the Carleton County Jail was one of the area's earliest prisons.

"It really was like a medieval prison," Glen Shackleton said in a CTV interview. "A lot of people died and they were buried in the yard."

In his 2007 book *Haunted Ontario Revisited*, Terry Boyle describes how many of the people sent to this prison were actually innocent victims without discrimination for whether they were men, women, or children; that they were seldom allowed to shower, rarely saw daylight, were fed a modicum of a daily meal, and many died as a result of social prejudice against the mentally ill and the poor. Their bodies were either burned or buried in the courtyard.

The ninth floor of the building, which used to be the hospital area, was converted into the location where women and children were crammed in. Young boys were jailed in that location until they reached the age of twelve, at which point they would be moved downstairs into the regular cellblock. Ghostly voices of children and the petrified screams of women are often heard on this floor by people working in the building as well as those who have stayed there.

Sharon Anne Cook writes, in her 2012 book *Sex, Lies, and Cigarettes: Canadian Women, Smoking, and Visual Culture, 1880–2000*, about a woman code named "Polly" as representative of one of the poor, intemperate, and certainly incompetent members of society. Marginalized by society, with little money for such things as food, clothing, and shelter, she would have been considered a person who belonged in the county jail. In Cook's study Polly is the face of poverty in late nineteenth-century Ottawa. A "vulnerable woman of the Canadian underclass," she was defeated, tired, and hopelessly trapped.

Women like Polly were, unfortunately, an all-too-common occurrence in the jail. One can imagine the spirits of hundreds of forlorn women like poor Polly still roaming the historic hallways of the ninth floor.

The Haunted Walks website contains a video that discusses a photo provided by one of the guests who had taken their "Ghosts in the Gallows" tour at the old Carleton County Jail. The photograph is of a glassed-in wall display of a large punishment ledger from the jail. Reflected in the glass you can see the woman taking the photo, holding her phone up in "camera aim" position. Beside her is the reflected face of another woman. The photograph came with a note from the photographer that reads: "I am on the right holding the camera. No one was in the room with me at all."

Female inmates at Carleton County Jail, February 1895.

Library and Archives Canada, Topley Studio, PA-0257437.

The woman who took the photograph described how she had decided to go in the cell alone to check it out. She'd felt a sudden chill down her spine and the cell felt cold. When she turned to look behind her, thinking that her father, who was also on the tour, had been playing a trick on her, there was nobody there. Then she turned back around to take the picture of the book. It wasn't until after she had taken the photo that she had spotted the figure beside her.

Jasmine, the tour guide at the time, relayed that the woman had broken away from the main group and had been alone at the time in question. Jasmine also pointed out that the face in the photo did not match any of the participants on the tour that night, nor was there anybody wearing a scarf or trench coat, which is what the "lone woman" reflection seems to be wearing.

As part of their followup investigation, Haunted Walk examined the multiple reflective surfaces in the cell and then attempted to recreate the photo using both an iPhone and an SLR camera, with the photographer standing in the same position and a colleague standing beside them, trying to be reflected in the same way. The results of both tests were quite similar to the original photograph.

So, while it was possible that the woman could have captured another person standing beside her, she was adamant that she was alone in the cell at the time.

The reflection of the strange "lone woman" remains a mystery, but it is certainly not hard to imagine that the woman caught reflected in the glass was one of those poor lonely souls forever trapped to roam the halls in spirit form.

In 2005, an Australian school teacher had been in the bathrooms on the fourth floor when she noticed a woman wearing only a blanket that she used to cover her head. As she approached her, and as the woman turned, the teacher saw that the woman had no face.

Hooded apparitions like that and other ghosts are also regularly seen in one of the more morbid locations: death row. Visitors have sworn they have spotted a figure in a long black cloak moving down the hallway, only to disappear.

There was an incident involving the director at the Haunted Walk. He was standing next to a heavy wooden door, conducting tours from one side of the building to another, waiting for the next group to arrive. While waiting, he heard three heavy knocks.

In surprise, he turned and opened the door. On the other side of the door another guide was standing several feet away with his own group of guests. Everyone in the party was looking at him in fright, eyes as big as saucers. One of them asked if he had been responsible for the loud knocking they'd just heard.

An underground tunnel that leads to the courtyard next door holds many dark secrets, but releases some of them in the form of echoing howls of prisoners that were tortured in their dark depths whose cries are still reported to this day.

There is a back stairway, known as the secret staircase, that is connected to the governor's house and considered one of the eeriest places of all. Prisoners told of the "ghost vampire" that lurked in this area and tried to "push the body out of your soul."

In 1972, when the jail was being restored, they found an inscription on the wall in the stairwell. It read: "I am a non-veridical Vampire who will vanquish you all. One by one I will ornate your odorous flesh with famished fangs. But Who? Are there 94 or 95 steps to the 9th floor? A book on the top shelf will lead you on the right path."

After one of the wardens had moved into the governor's mansion, one of his children, an eight-year-old boy, was allegedly possessed by the vampire ghost and he got sicker and sicker and his personality continued to change over time. He also developed an abnormally sensitive fear of the dark.

One might consider this to be the effect of a vampire ghost, or it might merely have been the symptom of the horrid conditions and the day-to-day atrocities that occurred in the jail. People committing crimes, from petty thieves to hardened criminals and murders, families who fell into debt, and scheming jail-breakers inhabited the overcrowed jail at the same time. Children as young as seven years old were housed alongside career criminals. People arrested under "drunk and disorderly" charges were thrown in beside the rapists and murders. Both the sane and insane were thrust together and in the madness, and lack of sanitation and proper shelter from the elements, it would be easy to see how anybody close in any way to this might suffer from such a deep and dark personality change.

A 1909 article from the *Ottawa Citizen* called attention to the plight of the insane in jails.

> Lack of room in the insane asylums is said to be the reason for keeping an insane woman since last August in the local county jail. The fact that she has been held there so long has caused considerable discussion among the officials. It is contrary to law to commit a person who is insane to a jail unless the patient is dangerous and then only for a short time.

In 1945, mayor Stanley Lewis said at a Board Control meeting, in a plea to move the jail out of the city and into the country, that "Carleton County Jail is a relic of the dark ages. The day has passed when offenders of the law are merely shut up and left to moulder away. Steps should be taken to help such people and reclaim them."

After yet another prison-break attempt in 1946, a Mr. O.A. Beach, foreman of the Grand Jury, issued a recommendation for a new courthouse and jail. He said he believed the attempt was primarily due to the inadequacy of the county jail, a museum piece that was regularly uncomplimentarily compared to Noah's Ark.

In 1965, Controller Kenneth Fogarty said that the county jail was very depressing and first offenders awaiting trial were often put in along with the hardened criminals. "One wouldn't do this sort of thing to an animal," he said.

In 1969, the jail was described in a newspaper article as being "medieval, grossly inadequate" and below the limits of human decency, with nothing being done about the incredibly cramped cells and lack of proper lighting, ventilation, plumbing, and privacy. A visiting jury described the visitor's room, the kitchen, and the dining room as appalling.

People who have stayed over in the hostel have reported waking up in the middle of the night and finding the apparition of a man holding a Bible either standing next to or sitting on the end of their bed. When describing him, they often describe a man who matches the description of Patrick James Whalen.

Whalen was charged and convicted of the murder of Thomas D'Arcy McGee, which occurred in the wee morning hours of April 7, 1868. Whalen's trial and conviction has been the subject of much debate, and Whalen himself protested the charges and proclaimed his innocence right up until the end.

When sentenced, Whalen turned to the judge and decried: "And yet all that, my Lord, does not make me guilty," with respect to the lack of solid evidence presented throughout the trial.

On February 11, 1869, more than five thousand people showed up in the midst of a horrible winter storm to watch Whalen hang. Whalen's last words to the crowd, just before dropping through the gallows trapdoor, were: "I forgive all those who have wronged me, I forgive all those I have wronged. God save Ireland and God save my soul."

Whalen was hanged at eleven o'clock on the 11th of February, 1869. Superstition dictates that a person ought to be hanged on the thirteenth hour of the thirteenth day of the month — thus, Whalen was two days and two hours early. He was also said to have been buried with the noose around his neck — the noose is supposed to be burned. And, finally, he was buried on prison property. If those three elements weren't enough to curse

Courtesy of N.D. Wilson.

The gallows in the early 1900s, as viewed from what is now Nicholas Street.

the very grounds the jail stands on, Whalen's final request that he be buried in his family's plot in a graveyard in Montreal was ignored. A devout Roman Catholic, Whalen allegedly said that if he were not buried in the proper way that no grass would ever grow over his grave. But Whalen's body was not moved to Montreal. Instead, he was buried in an unmarked grave that is most likely under the hostel's parking lot today. Interestingly, the man's prophecy regarding no grass growing over his grave came true.

Given the curse and the circumstances surrounding Whalen's death, many believe that his ghost is one of many haunting the building.

The gallows as seen from across Nicholas Street in the fall of 2015.

The hostel at night, winter 2015.

An empty cell from the Old Carleton County Jail.

Not all of the ghosts in the building are merely spectres that appear. Some have made their mark on those who enter the building.

One day a hostel staff member was up in the halls near death row when a heavy steel door slammed shut on her hand entirely on its own. The force was so great that it cut one of her fingers clean off. Another staff member, in front of several colleagues, felt a sudden hard slap coming from an invisible hand. As she stood there, aghast and confused, those around her saw a hand-shaped red mark start to appear on her face.

During a school group tour in 2003, two boys started goofing around and jumping up and down on a concrete slab that they were convinced Patrick James Whalen was buried under. In the midst of their laughing and jumping they suddenly stopped, their eyes wide and round and their laughter caught short in their throats. When they turned to face the rest of the group, everybody could see that they had both developed nosebleeds at the exact same time. Occasionally, when being told that story in the jail, a guest on the Haunted Walks tour will experience their own nose bleed. I know that during that part of the tour I took a second glance at Liz and also touched my fingers to my own nose to check, just in case. We were, of course, both fine.

Physically, at least.

When we left the building my mind filled with thoughts of the atrocities that took place there — the torture, the unofficial and illegal executions, the horrid living conditions, and the many tales of eerie incidents that so many have experienced over the years — I was happy to get back out into the cold fresh air of the Ottawa night.

We took one last walk around the side of the building to view the outside of the jail from the parking lot, and I felt a series of chills as I looked up at the windows and worried that any of the shadows I saw moving through them might not be those of hostel guests, but perhaps were shadows of the prisoners who might have physically escaped the hell of the prison but whose souls are trapped there forever.

A Horrific Thirty-One Days

The previous chapter explored the ghosts and historical conditions of the Ottawa Jail, but the deplorable conditions faced by inmates is something that can, all too easily, be overlooked when focusing on the more prominent elements of hauntings. Without mention of any spirits or hauntings, this account certainly qualifies as illustrating just how creepy our capital can be.

Below is an extensive article that appeared in the *Ottawa Citizen* in 1915, in which a man by the name of John Lyons, who had been imprisoned for thirty-one days at Carleton County Jail, spoke out about the terrible conditions. He writes quite eloquently and in great detail about the absolutely abhorrent conditions that he witnessed.

And yet, despite this eloquently written and exhaustive detail so early in the jail's history, it remained open and unchanged for another fifty-seven years.

In Carleton County Jail for 31 Days
John Lyons Summarizes His Experiences in Castle Dawson and Tells of Alleged Conditions There.

John Lyons, who was released from Carleton County Jail Thursday, has written of his experiences while undergoing a month's sentence under the caption

"Renewed Impressions of the County of Carleton Jail." His article follows:

Conditions have not improved noticeably since I was there two years ago.

The basic principle dominating the whole establishment is still punishment, not reform.

It functions primarily — it seems to me — as a sort of state incubator — a social hot-house, as it were, for the creation and maturing of criminals.

I came out worse than I went in, i.e., a less desirable citizen. Not the slightest attempt was made to show me — while there — the justice or expediency of our present system of land-ownership.

I am more determined than ever to do what I can to hasten the day when the earth and the fullness thereof shall be socially owned; i.e. our common heritage, and when the very idea of punishment — human and divine — shall be a thing of the past.

The insane are still confined there, temporarily — pending medical examination at the mercy of any degenerate who cares to torment them, and subject to an almost unthinkable cruelty on the part of the guards.

Abhorrent Conditions
There is a young man there serving his third term for vagrancy — six months — nine months — and six months — with hard labor, who is so unsound mentally that he has to be washed and dressed like a baby, yet he is out on the stone pile every day. Left to himself he is harmless, apparently, but when others torment him he becomes a perfect demon.

Confining the insane in the ordinary prisons is not fair to the guards, the other prisoners, or to the insane themselves; moreover, it is a direct contravention of existing law.

Mrs. Lyons and I — in defence of our children and as a public protest against what we considered an unjust law broke one of the laws, and were held up — by both Jude Gunn and Magistrate Askwith — to the scorn and execration of all "right thinking citizens," but Magistrates O'Keefe and Askwith, Chief Ross and Governor Dawson are permitted to break the law with impunity. Of course, ours was a breach of the law relating to property, while theirs is an infraction of the law relating to human life, which may explain the difference in results.

I found one of the "bailiffs" in there, whom I had formerly "obstructed." He is "doing" six months with hard labor for some offence. He had also served two terms at Kingston and one at Guelph. He told me of another of my bailiff "friends" whom I had similarly "obstructed" who is serving a nine months' term at Guelph.

Feeble-Minded There

There was a young English lad in the ward I was in, a boy of seventeen — an epileptic — whom Magistrate Askwith had sentenced to a month with hard labor for some petty theft. He would take fits at night and fall out of his bed. His heart-rending screams as the seizure came on him was sure to waken every prisoner in the ward. After that we were able to follow the progress of the attack by the every-changing sounds proceeding from his cell; the fall, the clatter of head and limbs on the floor as the muscles of his body were convulsed, the awful gasping, gurgling, choking sounds as the climax was reached, followed by the deep guttural breathing of the ensuring stupor which eventually changed into a form of hysteria during which he would cry for his mother. The whole affair was ghastly in the extreme and was always sure to put sleep out of the question for us for the rest of the night. In fact, my own nerves got in such a state that they would keep me awake often in anticipation of an attack. As Dr. Arguo — the prison doctor — said when he first saw him; — "Some day they'll send chaps like him to the hospital instead of to gaol."

There is a girl only seventeen in there at present, serving her second six months' term for loving "not wisely but too well." It would almost break one's heart to listen to her crying.

A Young Man's Lot

Perhaps one of the most unique cases is that of a young man who failed in business shortly after the war broke out, made an assignment to his creditors, liabilities, $500, assets, $400, and was thinking of going to Montreal where he had been offered a good position. This intention on his part was construed by one of his creditors — one to whom he owed $107 — as an attempt to "defraud," and he had the young man arrested, committed to gaol and has kept him there nearly three months, and so far as I can learn, is likely to keep him there the rest of his life. In reality he is being punished for a crime which he might possibly have committed had he not been so punished, which is surely a concrete illustrations of the "golden rule", i.e. "Do the other fellow or he'll do you, and do him first."

The day I entered, when my clothes were taken from me, I was permitted to retain a pocket handkerchief — to wipe away my tears with — also a tiny pocket looking glass, that I might see how much I failed each day. A safety-pin, found that same day, was helpful to me in keeping my teeth and finger nails clean. The principal viands on the bill of fare are "skilly", "black-stamp" and bread. I was compelled at the very start to discard the skilly, as my stomach revolted at it, and during the second week I had to do the same with the black-strap. The bread was good, but the Bible is where it says: "Man shall not live by bread alone."

We also had a taste of meat each day for dinner, except Sunday, and some fairly good pea-soup for dinner Wednesdays and Saturdays. The meat, I understand, is the refuse from a line of butcher shops in the city; meat that has been exposed in the windows and on the counters, until it is no longer sale-able, when it is sent down to the prisoners to eat. They don't get enough of it to hurl them though.

The Cooking Arrangements
One of the prisoners does the cooking for the rest, with another prisoner to help wash what they call the dishes. No knives or forks are allowed.

Sunday mornings we had a superfluity of religious services, when we were told with endless repetition about God's wonderful love for us; the eternal torments of hell, etc. Then for dinner we were served with a piece of dry bread and two or three dirty looking potatoes boiled with their skins on. We had those potatoes every day for dinner, but I could never eat them. The meat was always beef — boiled — and Roman Catholics had to eat it on Friday or make their dinner on dry bread and potatoes.

During the religions services was about the only time we could tell there were girls or women in the building, as we could then hear their sweet voices warbling — "Tell me the old, old story," "I love Thee because Thou has first loved me," "I need Thee, oh, I need Thee" etc. They could beat the men at singing. Our singing was not up to much, although the Catholics sang better than the Protestants. The last Sunday I was there the Salvation Army held a service which no one attended. The men seem to be about "fed up" with the organization, at any rate. Occasionally we could hear a woman screaming and moaning as though she were being beaten, but not often.

I had no difficulty — thanks to the kindness of friendly citizens — in getting all kinds of reading matter sent in to me, with the exception of the daily papers, and a Toronto weekly. I don't know whether the governor considered the latter too good or too bad for us, but it was held up at any rate.

Grand Jury Inspection
The members of the grand jury made their official tour of inspection through the gaol while I was there. They were ushered into our ward early one morning and proceeded to disport themselves around the ward in so aimless and lackadaisical a manner than some of us thought they were a fresh bunch of prisoners, and my young English friend came nearly asking one of them what he had been "pinched for." They were accompanied by the governor and one of the guards, and before they left their spokesman said to me: "Well Mr. Lyons, how do you find things in here?" I replied that I did not care to express myself on that subject while I was still in there. He smiled and said, "Perhaps it would be better not to," and added, "You certainly are not afraid to tell them what you think of it when you get out." (If he comes to me now, I'll give him all the information I can as to conditions in there.)

We asked "Scotty" the cook's helper that night if they had gone through the kitchen, and his answer was, "Oh yes, they went over the whole shooting match, merely as a matter of form." I haven't had the privilege of reading their report yet, but I fancy Scotty was about right. They were shown a spotlessly clean white enamel bath tub in our ward, but they did not discover that it had been out of commission for months, owing to a broken or detached pipe. Nor did they ask to have our cells unlocked, that they might inspect our beds, although the smell of them was nauseating, and the bed bugs got into our drinking cups at night and soiled our drinking water. My bed was particularly disgusting, owing to the fact that an insane Russian had occupied it for over a week prior to my incarceration, whose mental distress was so serious that he was unable to get up at night to respond to the calls of nature. After I had used it nineteen nights, I was given a clean, newly filled mattress, but the filthy blankets I had to use until the end of my time. Our pillow covers were changed once a week. The kitchen is alive with cockroaches, but it would be a safe bet that they didn't see any. The ventilation arrangements are so simply "rotten," and it must be a veritable pest house so far as disease is concerned, owing to the stench and the vermin. One razor serves all the prisoners, and occasionally it is given on literally covered with human blood. There are prisoners who seem to be dying with consumption; others with sores and ugly looking rashes, etc., but all use the same towels.

The Guards

The guards are a queer lot — some of them men who would think nothing of beating a poor insane fellow being, unmercifully, yet would object to the prisoners having an innocent game of checkers on Sunday as "a desecration of the Sabbath." They are preferable according to the shortness of their term of service there. One has been there a few months — another a few years, and a third — the worst of all — has been there twenty-seven years. The guards in my opinion, should be changed or relieved, every year, owing to the hardening, brutalizing, dehumanizing influence of their work and environment.

Requests of prisoners are constantly being refused on the grounds that they are "against the rules," but no one, except the guards, seems to have any idea what the rules really are. I think it would be only reasonable to supply the prisoners with a copy of the rules when entering. Then some are allowed privileges which are denied to others, and a request which is granted pleasantly enough one day may be received with curses the next. "May I use the phone, Mr. Young?" asked the young man, one day, who is being punished in anticipation of his evil deeds. "Blast you, No," followed by a torrent of oaths and personal abuse, was Mr. Young's reply. Prisoners are permitted to read by the governor, and are allowed to talk to a visitor — through a close wire netting, and in the presence of the governor and two or three of the guards — for five minutes each Friday.

It was a long month — thirty-one days and nights; seven hundred and forty-four hours; forty-four thousand, six-hundred and forty minutes; two million, six hundred and seventy-eight thousand, four hundred seconds.

Four Lights, Four Days

Mr. Robert Cummings, who appears in another chapter of this book in a story about an old haunted log house on his farm, is at the centre of this chapter as well, in a story pulled from the August 6, 1932, issue of the *Ottawa Citizen*. It is an odd, cautionary tale of a prophetic warning, perhaps fitting for an episode of *The Twilight Zone*, but intriguing nonetheless.

> **Four Lights On Grey Horse; Four Days Later Son Killed**
> *Strange Story Told by Mr. Robt. Cummings as to Weird*
> *Experience of His Mother in Nepean Some 35 Years Ago.*
> *Declared Queer Sight Was a "Warning." Son Was Killed*
> *By the Kick of a Horse.*

> In another column on this page Mr. Robert Cummings of Nepean tells a story of how the family dog laid a ghost about 40 years ago [to rest]. But Mr. Cummings also tells a more serious story which involved a "warning" of a death in the Cummings family. The story had an indirect connection with the old so-called haunted house referred to elsewhere.
>
> In the cellar of the old house Mrs. James Cummings Sr. used to keep butter and milk and things, as the cellar was very cool. One fall night about 35 years ago the

mother of Mr. Robert Cummings, having run short of butter in the house, went over to the cellar of the log house nearby to get a supply.

She told that as she came within 50 feet of the old place she saw a strange sight. There ran past her a dapple grey horse, which she had never seen before. But the peculiar part of the thing was that on the side of the animal next to her were four little lights. The lights were about the size of flashlight bulbs but were no so bright. They gleamed more like phosphorescence. They were in a line. The horse passed quickly. Mrs. Cummings was so disturbed by the sight that she returned to the home without getting the butter. At supper time she told of what she had seen. Of course everybody laughed and there were all sorts of explanations for the lights.

Didn't Laugh Later

But the family did not laugh four days later. In the afternoon of the fourth day after Mrs. Cummings had seen the dapple grey horse with the four lights, her son Joseph was killed from the kick of a horse. Mrs. Cummings then firmly declared the thing she had seen a "warning" and nobody disputed with her.

The story was widely discussed by the neighbourhood.

Screams from the Courtyard

Ghosts often reside in places with a long history, or where tragedy befell. Some locales, more than others, have had their share of tragedy and a long and interesting history of being a place where people congregated and came together for various functions and purposes. Such is the case with what is now a prestigious restaurant located in the heart of the market in downtown Ottawa.

The building at 21 George Street was built as a log tavern in 1827, designed to meet the needs of those who endeavoured to build Bytown into the city it would become. Within the first few years of the drinking establishment's existence, rooms were added onto the building and it was given the name McArthur House Hotel.

By the time the tenth anniversary of the building arrived, much of the original construction had been replaced by locally quarried limestone. During that time, the name also was changed to both the Ottawa Hotel as well as McArthur's British Hotel.

In 1865 construction of a new wing began, and that preceeded the building's lease to the federal government. One hundred and fifty men charged with protecting Governor General Lord Monck used the building as a garrison during the Fenian Raids between 1866 and 1870. The beautiful courtyard area that distinguishes the building today was the site of military hangings in the six years it was being used as a garrison.

Author's collection.

Ghosts often reside in places with a long history, or where tragedy befell. Such is the case with the prestigious Courtyard Restaurant.

After the military vacated the building, it became a hotel. A fire raged through it in 1872. A few years later, the building, refurbished and reconstructed, was reopened as the Clarendon Hotel. The attractive young daughter of the owners of the hotel laid a claim that she had been sexually assaulted by a young local MP. He was charged under the criminal code. During the trial he reported that her parents had tried to extort money from him in order to raise funds to support their ailing financial situation at the hotel. After a long and frustrating trial, the MP was exonerated but another shadow was cast on the building.

By 1880 the building became the headquarters for the Geological Survey of Canada and then became a branch of the mines department. During the typhoid epidemic of 1911 and 1912, the building temporarily housed a civil emergency centre, put in place in order to serve the residents of Lowertown. Then the mines department occupied the building until the middle of the Second World War.

The building sat vacant for many years until, in the late 1970s, renovations began to transform it into the Courtyard Restaurant, which opened in July of 1980. But a mere five weeks after the grand opening a fire in an adjoining building did enough damage that the new restaurant had to be closed for repairs. It was reopened in November of that year.

While there have been many tragic events over the years — including human trauma and lives cut short, which could all lead to many different restless spirits wandering the premises today — most of the stories lead back to one particular tragedy that occurred in the building.

In 1872, not long after the building had resumed its role as a hotel, a fire that destroyed a significant number of buildings on the block also affected the building at 21 George Street. While a handful of people were initially trapped in the flaming building, they all managed to eventually make their way down to the street and to safety.

A single woman by the name of Mrs. Evans was either unable to escape, or, after making it to safety, turned around and ran back into the building. There are differing accounts of the exact nature of what happened. But in all accounts, at one point, whether it was after she had escaped, or perhaps just while in the process of leaving, Mrs. Evans turned around, left the group of survivors she had been with, and returned to her room in order to fetch some personal papers that must have had some significance to her.

Those papers she was so adamant to retrieve resulted in her being trapped in the building. Witnesses to the fire, unable to go back in to help her due to the raging flames and thick black smoke, stood helplessly and listened to her screams echoing into the uncaring and bitter night air.

Staff at the Courtyard Restaurant have reported feeling uneasy and sensing some unseen presence in the building, particularly on the second floor. A very common uncomfortable feeling reported, typically when a staff member is by themselves, is an overwhelming sense that their presence is unwelcome. That something lingering within the walls of the building intensely wishes for them to leave.

Talk has long gone on about a powerful presence on the second floor, which, in addition to this ominous presence, also houses a private dining room and a loft. It can sometimes be a challenge getting staff to linger

Author's collection.

A Haunted Walks tour guide explaining the plight of Mrs. Evans in the devastating fire of 1872.

after hours to close the restaurant down, and some have admitted to having left personal items behind upstairs and deciding not to go back to fetch them out of a fear of being alone on the second floor.

In addition to the powerful presence reported by many staff members, others have reported lights turning on and off all on their own, as well as some of the electrical equipment at the bar starting up without anybody pressing the buttons.

Occasionally, on top of the feelings and odd flickering lights, the ghostly presence has also become visible.

A manager of the restaurant was closing up one night when she walked into the loft room on the second floor and spotted a woman in Victorian dress standing in the farthest corner of the room, gazing out the window. Startled that anybody was still there, the manager stepped back, casting her glance quickly around the room to see if anyone else was up there. When she returned her gaze to where the woman had been standing, she saw that the woman had completely disappeared. It wasn't until a few years after that a different staff member was up in the dining area of the second floor and spotted this very same apparition, dressed in the same old-fashioned Victorian garb, looking out a different window. This staff member reported that the woman was looking out the window and didn't move or acknowledge her presence in the room at all.

One particular member of the restaurant staff was skeptical and believed that the stories being shared were perhaps part of some sort of practical joke or initiation ritual, designed to frighten new staff, or just the result of overactive imaginations. She happily took as many late-night shifts as she could — particularly since many of the veteran staff members would happily switch shifts so they wouldn't have to be in the building in the quieter hours, late at night. For the longest time she was content with her extra shifts, and had never felt any sort of presence or experienced any of the other incidents shared through whispered tales in the kitchen. However, one night when she was closing and was on the second floor, she heard the sound of footsteps from the hallway coming toward her. When she went over to see who it was, there was nobody there; but the sound of footsteps continued, made by something unseen, and she felt someone brush up against her as the footsteps clearly moved right past her down the hallway. At that point, she headed downstairs, walked into the kitchen, and retrieved the largest knife she could find, sat in the middle of the floor with it clutched in her hand, and called her boyfriend to come and pick her up.

This beautiful restaurant in a gorgeous historic building remains a popular spot for romantic dinners, boasting an elegant atmosphere and fine foods prepared using meat and produce sourced fresh from local farms. Having celebrated thirty-five years of serving the Byward Market, the restaurant is the perfect mix of modern sophistication and old-world charm. The Courtyard's modern longevity is perhaps a nod to the intriguing and powerful history in which the building itself has played a part.

The Witch of Plum Hollow

There's an old empty log cabin that sits on the shores of Lake Eloida which people have always been drawn to. That's because the cabin is said to have once been the home of a famous witch.

Once upon a time, in a forest not far from Ottawa, there lived a lady by the name of Mother Elizabeth Barnes. She was also known as the legendary Witch of Plum Hollow. And the world beat a path to the woman's small log cabin door.

Mother Barnes used to consult with folks from the town, with politicians seeking advice, with farmers who had lost animals, and others who looked up to her for all the things that she could see and help them to better understand about the world.

But Mother Barnes was not actually a witch. She was a soothsayer, a clairvoyant, a water dowser, and a fortune teller.

She was also a mother, a grandmother, and a daughter — the seventh daughter of a seventh daughter, which, she claimed, is what gave her the "second sight" that she possessed.

Born Jane Elizabeth Martin in County Cork, Ireland, her father was an Irish landowner of English descent and a colonel in the British Army. Her mother was an Irish lady of Spanish Gypsy descent. When her father arranged her marriage to a man who was twice her age, twenty-year-old Elizabeth was distraught, as she was in love with a much younger man by the name of Robert Joseph Harrison. As the wedding neared, Harrison came to get her in the middle of the night and the two of them quietly slipped away, eloping to North America.

When Elizabeth's parents found out, they disowned her. But she was not phased. She was in love with her husband and delighted when they were blessed with a son, Robert Jr.

But when she was only twenty-seven, her husband died. She mourned his loss while struggling to raise their son on her own. But, being young, Elizabeth eventually met another man, and four years after her husband died she married David Barnes, and together they had nine children. In the fall of 1873 they moved to Sheldon's Corners near Athens, Ontario, and it must have been around then that she first discovered her special gift. This was also about when the nickname of "Mother Barnes" arose.

Two of their oldest sons died as young children, and Robert Jr., her first son, joined the U.S. Army, became a colonel in the Civil War, and died in Kansas.

Her husband David lost his interest in farming and moved to nearby Smiths Falls with their youngest son.

With a house full of mouths to feed, Elizabeth used her gift for fortune-telling in order to support her family. Once word got out, people started to trek to her home to have their fortunes told. They usually paid twenty-five cents or less for this.

When a reporter arrived to interview her, he coined the term "Witch of Plum Hollow." It was not meant to be a derogatory term, but the title stuck over the years.

Among the many achievements she was known for are finding the body of Morgan Doxtader and revealing that it was his cousin Edgar Harter who murdered him. Another man who had lost several sheep came to her to find them and she reported that he would find the meat in a barrel in his neighbor's cellar and that the hides were tacked on the neighbour's stable.

Lera Joynt, one of the descendants of Mother Barnes, said in a 1982 newspaper interview that the family didn't like the title of "witch" at all. "Her kindly advice and honest predictions helped countless numbers of people."

Elizabeth Barnes was buried in an unmarked grave in the Sheldon Cemetery. However, Claude and Ella Flood, local cheesemakers who'd lived in the community for fifty years, erected a headstone at the previously unmarked grave.

The Witch of Plum Hollow had been used as the title of a book by Thad Leavitt, a musical show produced in Toronto, and an oil painting by regional artist Henry Vyfinkel. Mother Barnes was also regularly written about in the *Ottawa Citizen*, particularly in a series of articles that reflected back on interesting and sometimes paranormal-related stories from the region's past.

Below is an article from the "Old Time Stuff" section of the *Ottawa Citizen* from February 8, 1935, that tells a tale of the woman's ability to see the future.

Recalled Uncanny Prediction When Close To Death's Door
Dave Farmer Didn't Believe Witch of Plum Hollow Could tell Fortunes But Now Testifies To Her Marvellous Powers, Her Prediction That He Would Travel To Another Country and Have Narrow Escape From Death Came True. Told Him What He Was Thinking About.

It is a long time since O.T.S. has presented any stories about that remarkable woman, "Mother" Barnes, the witch of Plum Hollow, who had an international reputation for telling fortunes and solving mysteries. She startled and mystified people by some of the things she told. O.T.S. has had various striking stories about Mrs. Barnes in the past, but most of them have been hear say. This week we present a story related by David Farmer, of Cumberland, who had actual contact with Mother Barnes in his youth, and who says her fortune telling his his case was positively uncanny.

For the benefit of those who may not have heard of Mother Barnes, let it be told that she resided in a small log house on the edge of Plum Hollow, about three miles from the town of Athens. As a fortunate teller, she was in a class by herself.

Could Read Minds.
Well, one day in the late seventies, Mr. Farmer and a number of companions decided to pay Mother Barnes a visit. But before entering the house Mr. Farmer had avowed his disbelief in the old lady's ability to tell fortunes by reading tea leaves. When they entered the shack she looked him steadily in the eyes and said:

"So you don't believe the old woman can tell your fortune, eh?"

Now the startling point of it all is that she did tell his fortune, and everything she told him turned out exactly as she predicted. She told him that he was going to travel to another country and be away from home for a long time, and that while he was away he would meet with an adventure that would end in his almost losing his life.

Was Shot Down.
Years later, after he had forgotten the old lady's gloomy prediction, Mr. Farmer found himself out in Butte, Montana. As he was walking down the street one dark night, carrying $2,700 in an inside pocket and sporting a valuable gold watch, he was attacked by two thugs, who requested his possessions.

When he showed fight, one of them opened fire with a revolver. One bullet passed through his left shoulder and the other grazed the side of his head. Had it not been for the timely appearance of a policeman, who scared the thugs away, he would probably have forfeited not only his belongings, but his life as well. As it was, he suffered untold agonies from his bullet wound for weeks after.

The "Old Time Stories" editors certainly enjoyed bizarre tales, and the one shared below from the February 8, 1936, *Ottawa Citizen* is unique and involves Mother Barnes solving the case of a missing moose.

Mystery of a Missing Moose Solved by Old Mother Barnes

Trapper Had Tame Moose Which Disappeared and Owner Had Reasons To Suspect Foul Play. Told His Troubles to Witch of Plum Hollow Who Gave Him Explicit Directions Leading to Solution of Mystery. Story of the Early Seventies.

Old Mother Barnes, the famed witch of Plum Hollow, who has been missing for several months from our stories of strange happenings in by-gone days, is back with us again. She figures prominently in the following tale related by Hilaire Leger, who by this time is known to all O.T.S. readers as the eighty-five-year-old skater of Sandy Hill.

About sixty-five years ago Jack Renaud had a farm on the Black River, Upper Ottawa river district, and his hired helper was Paul Guenet, a former lumberjack. They were the only dwellers on the river front at that point. In the bush about two miles back of them, was a squatter by the name of McLaughlin, who lived in a small log shanty and spent most of his time hunting.

Prized Possession.

McLaughlin had a tame moose, which often wandered far afield but always returned to its friend and master. One day the moose disappeared completely and, although its tracks were traced by McLaughlin along the road leading to the Renaud farm, both Renaud and Guenet insisted they had not seen the animal. McLaughlin searched the premises but could find nothing that would cast suspicion on the pair, other than the fact that the animal's tracks on the then muddy road stopped at the Renaud farm.

Going back to his shanty and pondering the problem for awhile, McLaughlin finally decided to seek outside help. He went to Mattawa and fell in with a shantyman who advised him to go and tell his troubles to old Mother Barnes, the witch of Plum Hollow, who had an international reputation for solving mysteries.

Her Advice.

After paying a nominal fee to the old lady, McLaughlin told his story and then sat back while she consulted her cards.

"I see the whole thing," she said. "All you have to do is go back to the farm near your place and look into the river where it takes a bend just beyond the farm. There you will find the head of your moose. Then go to the nearest tanner in your district and he will tell you who sold the animal's hide to him."

Sure enough, when McLaughlin returned and searched the river at the point indicated, he found the head of the moose, weighted down with a stone. From the tanner he received the information that the hide had been brought to him by Renaud's helper. Faced with the incriminating evidence of his guilt, Renaud, rather than have any fuss, paid McLaughlin eighty dollars for the loss of his moose — and admitted that he and Guenet had enjoyed several fine moose steaks.

Though Mother Barnes was not in fact a witch, the name seems to have stuck through history. From the novels, articles, stage shows, and artwork, all the way down to the shared stories told in whispers regarding the amazing things that she did, she certainly left her impression upon Canada and the world.

Mother Elizabeth Barnes died at the age of ninety-one, leaving behind seven children, many proud descendants, and a legacy of kindness and love. She was known as a wise old woman who invested a great deal of time and energy into assisting the hundreds of people who flocked to her looking for help and for answers.

Lisgar Collegiate Institute

The ghost on the top floor of Lisgar Collegiate Institute was so well-known that students would regularly dare one another to sneak up to the fourth floor attic, sometimes even locking one another inside, terrifying them that they might encounter the ghost that lived up there.

One of Ottawa's better-known high schools and one of the country's best regarded public schools, Lisgar Collegiate was established at its present location in 1873, after moving around several times in the preceding years. In 1892 it became the first public secondary school to hire a female teacher, and in 1957 was the first school in Ontario to introduce a special program for gifted students.

Dozens of famous and influential people have graduated from the school, including Paul Anka (singer), Adrienne Clarkson (broadcaster and former governor general of Canada), Lorne Greene (actor), Peter Jennings (news anchor), Rich Little (impressionist), Naomi K. Lewis (author), Matthew Perry (actor), and Shelagh Rogers (journalist and broadcaster).

While such a large cast of people who have moved through the school are notable and have moved on to great success, the building seems to continue to possess at least one spirit that has been unable to move on.

When hearing whispered tales of the ghost that haunts the building, many students assume that the ghost is the spirit of Lord Lisgar, the man after whom the school was named and whose likeness is prominently displayed in the school's library. However, Lisgar, who served as Canada's second governor general from 1869 to 1872, never set a single foot in the building, and the honour of having the school named after him came well after his death.

Other theories regarding the haunting involve a female student who was standing outside the building on a winter day in 1935 when a sheet of ice slipped of the roof and struck her, killing her. The belief is that she haunts the school, keeping a watchful eye out from the fourth floor, nearest the roof, to make sure that the fate she met is not repeated for any other student. Students have claimed to have looked up at the single window of the fourth floor and observed what looks like a young girl staring out at them.

A third theory involves the tale of a custodian who spent a good deal of time up on the fourth floor attic. Apparently, in 1940 he fell from the roof to his death in full view of hundreds of students. Given that the man had been responsible for converting the attic space into a storage area, which had occupied a significant amount of his time prior to his death, people believe that it is his ghost who walks around those darkened corridors.

Originally used as a drill hall and rifle range for student cadets, the fourth floor has but a single window on it, leaving the storage space there mostly dark and dingy. It has been described as laden with cobwebs, old uniforms, laboratory equipment, and even a human skeleton no longer being used in the biology lab.

The feeling of being watched is one of the most common experiences people have shared regarding the fourth floor, whether it was the feeling that someone was looking down at them on the school grounds from a window, or it was the feeling of someone else being on the fourth floor when they were supposed to be alone. Some students reported seeing a wispy figure drifting across the floor.

In Memorial Hall of the institute there are plenty of plaques and memorials dedicated to the memory of former students and specific individuals who went on to die in various conflicts, including the First World War, the Second World War, the Korean War, and the Boer War. But perhaps the most talked-about memorial is the unofficial one; that single round window on the fourth floor that nobody can ever seem to forget.

The Ugly Idol

The following article was originally published in the *Leader-Post*, a newspaper from Regina, Saskatchewan, on January 3, 1907, and was presented in John Robert Colombo's 2004 book *The Midnight Hour: Canadian Accounts of Eerie Experiences*.

Ugly Idol Startles an Ottawa Lady
Mrs. Tate Opens Glass Box Left by Mysterious-looking Stranger and Gets Fright

OTTAWA, Jan 2 — A most remarkable little object, apparently half fish and half gorilla, was found yesterday evening by Mrs. R.C. Tate, 496 Rideau Street, under circumstances that almost rival some of the stories of Edgar Allan Poe. Certainly, the supposed merman is one of the most hideously grotesque little things that can be imagined, and to run across it as Mrs. Tate did, in the dark garret, would disturb the nerves of the boldest.

One glance at the horrid Chinese Idol, Hindu god, or whatever it is, and Mrs. Tate dropped it back into the glass box from which she had taken it and rushed down stairs in a condition bordering upon hysteria. Several of the neighbours rushed into the house upon hearing the cries, and it was some time before the ladies could look upon the savage semi-fish without a shudder. Stories were told of people in possession of such a replica of oriental religious value being mysteriously stricken down by unknown assassins, and Mrs. Tate refused to have the image in the house over night, remembering possibly the fantastic stories such as "Moon-Stone" and other tales where idols' ears and images' eyes played most important roles in the deaths of whole families. As a solution in the matter, the peculiar object was taken to *The Citizen* office, where it now is, and may be seen by the morbidly curious. Just what the thing is supposed to represent is a mystery — in fact, more than one man has believed it to be a real merman, half ape, half shark. The story of the find is a most interesting and peculiar one.

About a foot long, the merman's lower half is fish, with fully developed tail, and six perfect fins. The upper part is certainly petrified, and a perfectly formed human or ape-like body. The hands are webbed with fierce-looking claws, while the big head, wrinkled and fearful, is turned to one side with a most malignant leer. Sharp teeth appear in the gums and the body is covered with long hairs. Altogether the effect is absolutely horrifying.

"A year ago in February," said Mrs. Tate, in telling the finding of the object, "a tall, dark-eyed man, with black hair, wearing a slouch hat and long grey coat, came to the front door and handed in a long glass box, hermitically sealed and apparently filled with wood. 'Give this to the man who used to live here,' the stranger said, smiling. 'He will know what I mean.'" The box was taken in and put in the hall for a week. No one called for it, and the garret was finally its resting place, where it lay for almost a year.

During Christmas week, Mrs. Tate made a lot of passe-partout work, and yesterday decided to make one more for a friend, overlooked at Christmas. No glass was to be had, and the lady was in despair until she thought of the glass box upstairs, left by the stranger a year ago. A little trouble brought the box to light, now covered with cobwebs, but hermetically sealed as first seen.

Taking a knife, the six glass sides were removed, when a black, cloth-covered board was found, with something fastened to it, and wrapped in yards and yards of wool. The last fold was torn away and the frightful little grinning merman was seen in the dim light of the attic. Uttering a shriek, Mrs. Tate rushed down-stairs and the house was an uproar in a moment.

Why the strange man left the object for the former tenant, whose person left her recently, Mrs. Tate does not know; why the former tenant failed to call for his oriental idol, or whatever it is — all these points are a mystery.

The Mysteriously Protected Library of Parliament

The Parliamentary Library in Ottawa has survived some terrifically challenging odds, suggesting that there just might be something beyond this world that has allowed it to survive.

The fact that the library stands today, despite multiple disasters that threatened to destroy it over its long history, is a testament not only to the foresight of librarian Alpheus Todd and a library clerk, but perhaps also to some unseen presence that continues to guard the building.

Todd insisted both on the "chapter house" style design of the building, which kept the library separated from the main parliamentary buildings, as well as the iron fire doors that were part of the design. So on that fateful night of February 3, 1916, when the fire alarm sounded at 8:37 p.m., quick-thinking library clerk Connolly "Connie" McCormac ensured that the iron fire doors were slammed shut before evacuating the building.

The iron fire doors helped prevent the fire, which completely destroyed the main Parliament buildings, from spreading. The fire had allegedly spread from a smouldering cigar that had been tossed into a wastebasket, quickly catching on the recently oiled wooden interior walls and the just-varnished floors. A high wind coming in from the northwest caught the growing fire just west of the library and swept it

The Parliamentary Library as seen from near the entrance to the Rideau Canal, fall 2015.

Author's collection.

toward the senate. The bell in the Victoria Tower crashed to the ground, with witnesses reporting that the bell and tower were overtaken by flames only after completing the midnight chime. Men from the fire department worked throughout the night, valiantly trying to bring the disastrous blaze under control.

That historic night in 1916 wasn't the first time the library was threatened and it certainly wouldn't be the last.

A massive fire touted as "The Great Fire of 1900" started in a defective chimney on the Gatineau side of the Ottawa River and killed seven people, left fifteen thousand people homeless, and did an estimated $9.5 million in damage. A swath of flames consumed the mostly wooden homes of the city, from Lebreton Flats to Dow's Lake, destroying 14 percent of Ottawa homes and 42 percent of the homes across the river in Hull. The Parliament Buildings, and the Parliamentary Library, were spared from this devastating fire.

Early in the Library of Parliament's history, the Legislature and its library moved from Kingston to Montreal and then alternated between Toronto and Quebec City for several years, before finding a permanent home in Ottawa in 1857. The most disastrous blaze that threatened the library during that time was when a Loyalist mob protesting the Rebellion Losses Bill burned down the Legislature and destroyed all but two hundred of the twelve thousand books from the library.

In 1952, an electrical short in the roof of the library caused a fire that almost destroyed the entire building. Firefighters cut through the metal roof in order to put out the flames that were spreading beneath the library's dome, causing flood and water damage. But for the second time, the library itself survived any major disaster.

Was it blind luck or an otherworldly presence that has continued to protect the library from one of books' most devastating enemies? Could it be fearless librarian Alpheus Todd, continuing on his mission of keeping his beloved library safe? Perhaps a former politician, trapped forever in Parliament, keeping an eye on the Canadian treasures that the library holds.

The Ghost on the Lonesome Road

Earl George Wilson compiled a series of interesting, amusing, chilling, and entertaining reminiscences of Ottawa's "earlier days" in a back-page feature of the *Ottawa Citizen*. It was a popular feature that Wilson edited from 1932 to 1939.

Born April 1, 1891, Wilson died at the age of sixty-three in 1955 after a long and successful career as a reporter and editor.

Below is yet one of the more interesting stories that Wilson compiled and shared with fascinating *Ottawa Citizen* readers over the years. It involves an intriguing odd figure in a while sheet and the eerie spectre of a recently departed young man sitting on a fence on a lonely old road.

It appeared on July 16, 1932.

**Was It Ghost Of a Dead Youth That
Cummings Children Saw**
*Or Was Somebody Playing Prank on Lonesome Road
Near North Nation Mills in the Year 1854? A Story of
Believe It or Not Told by Old-timer Now Resident in
Cumberland Township.*

Like a lot of other people, Mr. Abel Watters Cummings, aged 85, of Cumberland township, enjoys reading the weird happenings of the past, as narrated by the Old Time Staff.

He says he only had one experience of the weird. That occurred when he was a boy of seven and lived several miles from North Nation Mills. He says he does not know whether someone was playing a prank, but anyway he received such a scare that he has never forgotten the incident.

In the summer of 1854 a young daughter of Alanson Cook of North Nation Mills had been staying at his home, and was to go from there to the home of Sam Cook, about three miles away. He (Abel Cummings) and his two sisters (the eldest aged 18) saw the girl over to Sam Cook's. When they left their home it was growing dusk.

Saw a White Figure

Before they reached the Sam Cook home it had become dark. When not far from their destination, they saw approaching them on the road a white-clad figure. As it passed them on the road they could see that the figure was clad apparently in a white sheet. The figure did not speak.

After whatever it was had passed, his (Abel's) eldest sister said to her younger sister, "That was a ghost we saw." The younger sister replied, "It must have been someone trying to frighten us."

"No," said the elder, "that was the spirit of _____ _____." She named a young man who had died several years before and who was 18 years of age at the time of his death.

The girls and Abel turned and looked down the road. The white sheeted figure was still in sight.

The incident provided talk till the Sam Cook home was reached.

Seen on Return Trip

On the return trip the two girls and Sam kept a sharp lookout for the spook. They did not see the figure again till their home was almost reached. Then they saw it again. The figure was sitting on the roadside fence. It did not move or even groan.

When they got home and told their story, their father said they must have imagined the whole story.

Mr. Abel Cummings says they undoubtedly did not imagine what they saw, as all four saw the same thing. It probably was somebody's prank. But if such was the case, why didn't the prank-player groan or anything?

Recalled Many Years Later

Mr. Cummings adds that 45 years later, while seeing his older sister at Calumet, he casually mentioned the incident of the ghost. To his surprise his sister recalled every detail of the incident just as his own memory had it. And she was firm in her belief that they had seen the ghost of young _____ _____. She had known the young man as a young girl and recognized his face.

"That was my only spook experience," said Mr. Cummings. "I give it for what it is worth."

Some Nightmares on Elm Street

Being in a new town, at a new school, and in a completely new environment can be nerve-racking enough. But when the experience is compounded with an overactive imagination and an odd series of eerie events, it can become overwhelming. And, under the right circumstances, it can lead to a plethora of tales I've been able to share around campfires or dimly lit rooms for the past quarter century.

When I first moved to Ottawa in 1988 to attend Carleton University, I was, admittedly, a nervous and frail young man. I had never lived away from home before and was fortunate that my cousin Rodney, who was going into his second year at the University of Ottawa, had room for a fourth roommate in a house on Elm Street that he had rented with two friends.

And so it was that I found my nineteen-year-old self in a two-storey, four-bedroom home located in Chinatown in Ottawa with my cousin and two beautiful young women, Nana and Maureen. For virtually any heterosexual young man, the situation of being roommates with two lovely young women like that might inspire thoughts and fantasies more akin to the pages of an adult magazine. But this particular young man, though cognizant of the appeal, was still coming to terms with the recent changes to his locale.

Some of the "Elm Street" gang. Left to Right: Rodney, the author, Maureen, Tammy, and Taki.

Not having spent more than a few days away from my childhood home, I remember finding myself in a surreal haze with several pieces of my relocated bedroom furniture in a city six hours east of the only place I had ever lived.

I remember how ultimately frightened I was that first night, when I went to bed in the new house. As I lay there in the dark, listening to the sounds of the city outside my bedroom window, I wondered how many different people had stayed in this very same room and what their stories were. I marvelled at that thought, as the idea of being in a room or house where who knew how many others might have lived before made it feel as if the very walls of the building might have absorbed stories and images from these countless unknown individuals.

One night during my first week at 5 Elm Street, I remember waking up and hearing a strange noise coming from downstairs. All of the other occupants in the house were asleep and I dashed out of my bed and ran to the light switch near the door to my room.

When I flicked the light on there was a sudden burst of brightness, then the room descended into darkness; a darkness far more pitch than it had seemed before, thanks to the sudden bright flash that had come when the light bulb in my room had gasped its final huge exhalation of light.

The light bulb burning out made me think back to the last person who had lived in this room. I wondered about the light bulb itself. How long ago had it been screwed into the ceiling in my room? And who had screwed it in? Where were they now? The light bulb going out, to me, represented a small death, the end of something that had gone here before. Yes, in the middle of the night and in the dark, my mind would often speculate about such mundane matters.

I opened my door and slipped into the hallway, where I turned the light at the top of the hall and stairway on.

I heard footsteps coming up the stairs, and a second later the top of someone's head appeared over the edge of the banister.

"What's the matter with you?" my cousin Rodney said to me as he ascended the stairs and saw me standing there in my pajama bottoms, my face pale and likely presenting a look of shock.

"Nothing," I muttered sheepishly, realizing that the sound I had heard had been him coming home from his shift as a bouncer at a pub on Elgin Street. "My bedroom light just burned out."

"There's a box of bulbs in the third drawer in the kitchen," he mumbled, entering his room at the top of the stairs. "Goodnight."

Rodney and I had grown up quite close together, his father and my mother being good friends. He was like a big brother to me, and I was thankful for his pragmatic nature and outlook. Because the minute I started to fall off the rails with my overly active imagination, Rodney could easily pull me back in.

Rodney, Maureen, and Nana, all of whom were in their second year of university, were friendly, welcoming, and accommodating. They were also aware of my lack of worldly experience and were patient with me as I slowly began to acclimatize myself to my new space in the world. It helped that I also knew Rodney's girlfriend Tammy from my former high school and that Maureen's boyfriend Taki was a friend of mine from that same high school. (Small world, indeed). The six of us enjoyed the three floors of our large home and did plenty of things together. The routine helped me to become accustomed to my new home and the new experience of attending my first-year classes at Carleton.

One night, sometime close to midnight, when the entire group of us (except for Rodney, who was working his shift at the Lieutenant's Pump) were all sitting around drinking beer and rum and coke, listening to music, talking, and laughing in the large dining room at the back of the house on the main floor, there was a knock at the door.

"We're not expecting anybody, are we?" Taki asked.

"Maybe Rodney forgot his keys," Maureen suggested.

Nana giggled nervously as Tammy got up and headed to the door.

"Maybe we were being too loud and some of the neighbours are here to complain," I said. The thought of that made me nervous. I was never one to want to disturb the balance or upset the peace.

"We're barely making any noise," Taki said, but at that point he reached over to the tape player and turned the volume down before getting up to follow Tammy to the door.

As I had been sitting at the end of the table farthest from the entrance to the hallway that led to the front door, I couldn't see anything.

But I heard Tammy mutter the word "pizza," before opening the door.

"Pizza," a male voice said. "Pepperoni and mushroom."

From around the corner, the distinct smell of pizza drifted in, making my stomach growl.

"We never ordered a pizza," Tammy said.

The male voice said something else that I couldn't hear, and then Taki spoke up. "Sorry, man, we didn't order a pizza. You must have the wrong house."

The door closed and we returned to our chatter, drinking, and laughing, and didn't think anything of it.

Until the next night, when it happened again.

Rodney was at work again, and Maureen, Nana, and I were sitting in the dining room just finishing a late supper that we had cooked together, when there was a knock on the door.

All three of us went to the door, where, again, a young man had been standing with a box of fresh pepperoni and mushroom pizza.

We all looked at one another, confused, before Maureen opened the door.

"Pizza delivery!" the young man at the door said.

"Sorry," Maureen told him, "we just finished dinner. We didn't order any pizza."

This time, the smell of the pizza wafting in from the doorway didn't entice my stomach the way it had the night before. Although it smelled just fine, there was something about it that turned my stomach.

After the young man, who was noticeably angry with the situation, left, the three of us went back to the dining room where we sat around the table and started talking about what had happened.

That had been two nights in a row that a pizza delivery person had showed up at the door to bring a pizza that nobody had ordered. Had someone been playing a practical joke on us?

We sat around the table, the dirty dishes forgotten, as we speculated about the nature of these nocturnal pizza-delivery visits. After finishing her night class at Carleton, Tammy arrived at the house and sat with us well into the night as we spoke about the incident.

Though it was merely strange and there should have been nothing to fear, some of our talk turned to the supernatural. And none of us wanted to go to bed, despite having early morning classes the next day.

Having talked through the situation for several hours, working the nervousness out of ourselves, eventually we all went to bed.

But a knock on the door in the middle of the night woke me up, and I lay in bed for a moment, petrified. I was pretty certain that, had I not heard Maureen, Nana, and Tammy already standing out in the hallway at the top of the stairs, I would have stayed tucked in beneath my sheets, quivering in the darkness.

But hearing that they were already up gave me the jolt of bravery that had evaded me a moment earlier, and I joined them out in the hall, and we all looked at one another.

"The pizza man?" one of them said.

"God, I hope not," I muttered.

And, though it was silly for us to be frightened at something as mundane as a pizza guy standing at our front door, something about it gave me the heebie jeebies. It apparently had done the same to the others as well.

The three of us descended in a tightly packed group down the stairs slowly, grabbing on to one another's arms for comfort and creeping cautiously to the bottom of the stairs. Our porch light was on, and as soon as we reached the bottom of the stairs, we could clearly see down the hall out to the front porch and the fact that there was nobody standing there.

We slowly moved toward the door, went right up to the large window, and looked out, to the right, down the steps. There wasn't even a car parked in the drive. There was no indication that anybody, pizza-delivery man or not, had been at our door.

And yet, we knew that we had all heard the knocking.

The four of us spent the next couple of hours sitting in the dining room with all of the lights on the main floor turned on, waiting for Rodney to get home from his shift at the pub.

When he got in the door he asked us what we were all doing up and we told him about the odd pizza deliveries.

Rodney looked at me, knowing I was the one with the fertile imagination, and said, "Now look what you've done. You've gotten everyone all worked up." Then he announced that he was tired and going to bed.

"But," Maureen said, "what if there's another knock at the door?"

"Don't answer it!" Rodney retorted and started heading to his room.

"Should we wake you if he returns?" I called after him.

"Not if you know what's good for you."

The rest of us eventually retired to our rooms and I remember being so frightened about the situation that I couldn't sleep. So, instead, I went to my computer, a Commodore 64 console that was hooked up to a small colour television on the desk in my room. It came with an external hard drive and I also had a nine-pin dot-matrix printer connected to it.

I spent several hours typing up a fictional story entitled "The Pizza Man," and the following morning, after everyone else in the household was awake, I printed the story out so I could read it to them. I changed our names and added fictional elements to each of our characters, as writers are wont to do, but maintained Rodney's pragmatic and no-bullshit manner. Everyone liked that aspect of the story the most.

In the fictional tale that I crafted, the situation is somewhat the same as what we had experienced, except I have all four of the students around for most of the recurring events. And, in the tale, they play a more active role in trying to determine why this mysterious figure keeps appearing at the door every single night from the very first night they had moved into their newly rented home.

Along the way, the students discover clues hidden in the basement that suggest an abduction and murder had taken place in the home before they had moved in; the name tag of a pizza-delivery boy has been found, and the students learn that, one year earlier, a student pizza-delivery person matching the description of the young man who keeps appearing at their door went missing in the middle of his shift. The entity mysteriously appearing at the door is none other than the now-dead pizza man, faithfully endeavouring to deliver the pizza to the last house on his route.

The story was published in my digital collection *Bumps in the Night: Creepy Campfire Tales*, and if you are interested in it, simply email me at mark@markleslie.ca and I'd be happy to send you a copy in either PDF or eBook format.

Shortly after I read the first draft of "The Pizza Man" to my Elm Street friends, the mysterious knocking at the door and delivery of unordered pizzas stopped. That's not to say pizza never came to our door, because we quite regularly ordered pizza; it is a staple food of students, after all. But every single other time a pizza man arrived at our door, it was from a pizza joint that we had consciously ordered from. And we never ordered a pizza with just pepperoni and mushrooms on it; the thought of that continued to give some of us chills.

Things resumed as normal in the student home. And then, somewhere along the way, Nana acquired a cat, a cute little black, grey, and white tabby that she named Spot.

Despite my allergies to dogs and cats, or perhaps because of them, Spotty found himself attached to me, and longed to spend a lot of time in my room. That was most likely due to the fact that I was at home more than any of the others, and so Spotty and I had that in common.

Even had I not been allergic to animals, I might have still had some trepidations about getting too close to the little furry creature. Animals, cats in particular, are apparently more in tune with things that humans typically are unable to observe. And, given my nervousness about the past tenants in the house, I didn't want to see the cat do anything that might make me think the house was haunted in any way.

I thus did my best, over the months, to ignore whenever Spotty would arch his back into the air as if some unseen hand was petting him, or whenever he acted strange and would, for no determinable reason whatsoever, suddenly alter his route when walking down the hallway, as if taking a quick jog around some object that wasn't there — or at least not that I could see.

And whenever he hissed or seemed to be staring off at something that he was apparently concerned about but which I couldn't see, I immediately thrust my nose back into the comic book I was reading, or turned up the television in the hopes of drowning out whatever it was he had been up to.

One night, in the middle of the cold Ottawa winter, I had been sharing tales with Maureen and Taki around the dinner table from a book I had been reading. I was midway through Jay Anson's *The Amityville Horror: A True Story* and had been telling them about a scene I'd recently read in which the main character was outside in the yard and had looked up at one of the windows to see the glowing pig-like eyes of the creature that his daughter, Missy, had apparently befriended.

Shortly after cleaning up their dishes, Taki and Maureen were heading over to Taki's place. Both Rodney and Nana were working, and, as often happened, I was alone in the house.

As they bundled up to make the walk over to Taki's place in the cold winter air, I ran upstairs and went into Rodney's bedroom, which looked down on the street, in order to make faces at them, as I regularly did. There was enough light coming in to the bedroom from the nearby streetlight that they could easily see me, and, in order to see them, I kept the lights in the bedroom off.

I was smiling and giggling as I stood there in the dark, wiggling my fingers with my thumb on my nose and watching them laugh.

Then, all of a sudden, Taki, who had also been laughing, got a very serious look on his face and called out something in a loud voice.

"What?" I called back, unlatching the window and lifting it so I could hear him.

"Behind you!" Taki called, pointing up at me. "In the dark behind you! Red pigs eyes!"

Taki then turned around, laughing hysterically. Maureen slapped him on the arm, saying, "Taki!" in a very disapproving voice, and the two of them walked up the hill and out of sight.

As for me, with the deepest of chills running down my spine, I stood at that window for several minutes, staring out at the street. Sure, I knew that Taki had been joking, but a part of me wondered if maybe he wasn't. I was simply unable to find the courage to turn, in case I might be looking into the red glowing eyes of "Jodie," the demonic friend from the book I had been reading.

I eventually mustered the courage to turn and leave the darkened bedroom; more likely the need to visit the restroom overtook my fear, and I spent the rest of the night waiting for Rodney and Nana to come home with virtually every single light in the house on.

Sometime in the spring, just as the cold Ottawa winter was winding down and the snow was melting, I remember lying in bed in the early morning hours and hearing an odd scratching sound coming from somewhere.

I remember looking for Spotty, wondering if it was him digging at the carpet near my door, as he would often do whenever my door was closed and he was eager to get inside, but I found him sleeping on the end of my bed.

But there was still that odd scratching sound, echoing through the dark.

The scratching occurred every single night, sometimes bothering me enough to prevent me from getting to sleep. And I was nervous about mentioning it to my roommates because they already knew that I had a hair-trigger imagination and affinity for jumping at shadows.

Nobody else mentioned any odd scratching sound that they could hear, so I didn't say anything, but there were plenty of times I would walk around on the second floor of the house and try to determine where the scratching was coming from.

It seemed to be coming from the ceiling.

I pushed aside thoughts of the spirit of some abducted and murdered soul that had been left in the attic to die (similar to the story that had helped me create "The Pizza Man") and started looking for a more logical and reasonable explanation for the sounds that had been plaguing me.

While frustrating at the time, at the very least that incident did inspire yet another short story that kicked around in the back of my head for a few years before I wrote it down. That tale, which was about a man who wakes in the middle of the night to discover tiny gnome-like creatures digging a tunnel into his home through the ceiling, was entitled "Little Things" and was published in the magazine *Necrotic Tissue* #13 in 2011, some twenty-two years after the incident that had first inspired it.

I eventually determined that the scratching was not some undead creature stuck in my attic, nor little gnome-like miniature men trying to dig their way into my life, but likely a squirrel or perhaps a mouse that had gotten in to the attic and made its nest.

Fortunately, despite the many, mostly self-inflicted, nightmares I experienced in my time at 5 Elm Street, I survived and came away with some fun and intriguing stories of my very first days in Ottawa that can often spark interest and chills in listeners and readers to this day.

Almost Scared to Death

Something almost as commonly shared as ghostly tales are stories that, like the plot of an episode of *Scooby-Doo* or a Hardy Boys novel, were actually completely manufactured.

Deserted old buildings, decrepit and boarded up homes, abandoned hotels, and theatres are ripe for the picking for such tomfoolery. Pranks can, of course, be fun and good-natured and, after their fright, can cause a laugh, often from a huge sense of relief.

But sometimes they can go too far, like when a shock causes someone enough fright that it almost kills them.

Below is an article from the March 29, 1929, *Ottawa Citizen*.

Weird Light in Old Cunningham Hotel Nearly Scared Farmer's Wife to Death
But in This Case the Spectre Light was Boy-Made-Story of "Haunted House" Near Gloucester Station in the Year 1874 — Doctor Had to be Called In — Woman in Bed Several Days

The country surrounding Ottawa has experienced many hard-to-explain incidents of a supposedly super-natural character. There have also been many cases of ghosts that weren't ghosts — sort of concocted ghosts.

For example there was the case in the seventies of the deserted Cunningham Hotel near Gloucester Station, which was supposed to be haunted, but wasn't. Mr. Thomas Graham tells a funny story about how a farmer and his wife were almost scared to death by a boyish prank in the old house in the year 1874.

Some of the older boys of the neighborhood who had heard of the stories of lights appearing in the empty house years before, decided to revive the spooks.

One dark night they went to the old hotel equipped with a lantern and a piece of white cotton.

Soft Weird Light.
Whenever a buggy or wagon approached the buildings, the boys threw the cloth over the lantern so as to produce a soft weird light and walked around the house with it so as to give the impression of a spirit rambling through the building.

The sudden reappearance of the lights caused a lot of talk in the township the next day.

In one case the lights caused a woman to get sick.

It appears that among those who passed the old hotel that night and saw the lights were a Frenchman and his wife.

As their buggy came near the building the wife said: "Do you think there are any ghosts in the old house."

Certainly Not.
The husband laughed heartily. Certainly there were no such things as ghosts, he said. And anyway no lights had been seen in the old place for many years.

Real Excitement.

As they looked at the old buildings, lights were seen moving round; weird lights, ghostly looking lights. The woman screamed and the horse started to run. The man let it run. In fact he made it gallop. As soon as the woman got inside her home she fainted. A doctor had to be sent for. The woman was in bed for several days with a bad attack of nerves.

When the boys heard of what had happened they discretely kept away from the old house.

Arnprior Ghosts

Arnprior is a small town in the Ottawa Valley at the junction of the Ottawa and Madawaska Rivers. Considered the gateway to tourism in the Ottawa Valley, with an abundance of walking, hiking, and biking trails, it is a quiet town known mostly for hydro generation, lumber, aerospace, and agriculture.

This town of just over 8,000 people is also known, in certain circles, to contain a few intriguingly eerie elements, such as a ghost in a cursed home and a haunted museum.

The Arnprior and District Museum is located in the town's former post office, which was designed by Thomas G. Fuller, the world-renowned designer of the original centre block of Parliament in Ottawa. Fuller's brilliant use of local materials in his designs ensured that his Gothic and Romanesque work was easily recognizable.

This designated heritage location has reported a few incidents that make people think that not only does this building bring the past to life, but perhaps someone from the past is still actively present in the building.

The Toronto and Ontario Ghosts and Hauntings Research Society reports an interview with a former volunteer at the museum, in which they describe a story they had heard about an old curator of the museum who lived on the third floor with his wife. He had apparently been abusive to her, and she ended up hanging herself in the basement. The basement, however, was never a spot where the volunteer had encountered anything weird. But they certainly encountered strange things in other spots in the building.

The volunteer shared a story in which they had been assisting a photographer with shooting pictures of a Victorian display. When looking at the photos afterward, they were startled to see, in two different pictures, the same body of a woman in black reflected in the glass. The reason it was startling is that there was nobody in the room wearing clothes matching what could be seen in the reflection.

The Aerendel website (www.aerendel.ca/haunted/Haunted02.html), run by a couple named Cathi and Jim, has similar photos of a couple of displays that have captured this exact phenomena. Of interesting note, in one of the photos not only does the figure in the black shirt appear in the reflection of the glass display case, but a woman's face also appears reflected in a nearby painting.

The volunteer at the museum relayed another story, in which they were on the second floor doing some work when they heard thumping, banging, and shuffling coming from upstairs — almost as if furniture was being moved. The noises continued and they started to head upstairs, wondering what the new temporary employee had been doing up there. As the volunteer walked upstairs, calling ahead, the noises of the shuffling and the bangs began to slow and then stopped completely.

"I hurried downstairs a bit freaked," the volunteer said, "and just as I got down there I heard the door outside open and the temp walked in and went up to do her work and no one was there."

Finally, the volunteer told a story of when they were working near the Victorian bedroom display when all of a sudden they heard what they described as a very loud, concentrated bang. They said it sounded and felt as if a bowling ball had been dropped immediately behind them on the floor. They immediately froze in shock, then quickly scooted for the exit, not wanting to see what was behind them. But as they fled, they glanced over their shoulder to spy that there was nothing or nobody standing there. They had been all alone the entire time. "I never felt threatened," they concluded.

†

The Old Grierson House in Arnprior is a two-storey home built in 1865 and once owned by Lieutenant John Grierson. Over the years the building has served in different roles, including a medical clinic and an inn. Legend has it that when the Old Grierson House was operating as an inn one wintry, stormy night, the innkeeper refused entry to a stranger who had been looking to come in out of the inclement weather. Being turned away, the stranger wandered back out into the blizzard and ended up freezing to death in the snowstorm. Ever since that fateful night, several tragic deaths that occurred in the building have been attributed to that event, almost as if there were a curse on the building itself. Inside, doors are known to shake on their own, chains are heard rattling in the basement cellar, an odd thumping is heard echoing down from the attic, and footsteps are said to be heard shuffling back and forth down the hallways.

Ottawa Museum of Nature

The official name of what most people know as the Ottawa Museum of Nature, a landmark building in the city of Ottawa, is the Victoria Memorial Museum Building. It is also known to many as "the castle." But just like there is a difference between the official name and the commonly used name, there are certainly different lights that the museum is seen in.

During the day it is a natural history museum, housing collections that started in 1856 with the Geological Survey of Canada and now including virtually any aspect of the intersection of human society and nature. But nighttime is further inspiration for nightmares, and perhaps a reminder that the displays seen during the day don't quite include all aspects of human society. After all, aren't fear and terror a fundamental part of our makeup?

The building's main architect and designer, David Ewart, created a structure that reflected the Romanesque and medieval styles common in Europe, while adding in Gothic and Tudor features. The building was also meant to mirror the structure and look of the centre block of the original version of Canada's Parliament Buildings. The building was the first of its kind to incorporate designs of Canadian animals into its carvings, featuring moose heads, beavers, and other animals native to the Canadian wilderness.

Employees of the museum have reported eerie sounds echoing down the halls at night, of elevators moving without anybody operating them, of doors opening and closing all on their own, and odd cold spots on the fourth floor.

One night a female employee of the museum watched in horror as what she described as the hollow outline of a man formed in the reflection of a mirror she was looking in, then passed right through her body. She claimed to have felt an extreme sensation of heat at that moment and was unable to move until the image finally vanished.

Many customers over the years have reported to museum staff that they have had the uncanny feeling of being watched.

The museum supposedly has trouble keeping security guards. After working a night shift and experiencing one of these spooky occurrences, many have turned in their resignation.

Remembering some of these facts from the first time I had gone on the Ottawa Haunted Walk tour, I stored the fact away and ended up using it in a story I wrote and had published in *Tesseracts Seventeen*, an anthology of exclusively Canadian-authored stories, in 2013. The story,

During the night, the Ottawa Museum of Nature is inspiration for nightmares rather than the intersection of human society and nature.

Courtesy of Haunted Walks Inc.

214

"Hereinafter Referred to as the Ghost," opens in this particular locale, and is told from the point of view of a ghost waiting to surprise an unsuspecting yet nervous security guard.

In an attempt to draw upon elements from the creepy tales I had heard, I wrote the following as the opening:

> Patrick Collins waited for the burly young security guard to walk past. Though it had been over five hundred years since he needed to bother hiding in shadows or behind objects — he could, after all, fade in and out of the visible spectrum at will — it was still something he did mostly out of habit.
>
> No, not just habit. Lately there was another reason.
>
> But he didn't want to think about that just now. There was a macabre task at hand.
>
> Patrick grinned darkly. He knew that this guard, a William Blakely, had been with the museum less than three weeks. This was his first night shift and he had indeed heard the stories about the corridor being haunted. That set just the right atmosphere for what Patrick had planned.
>
> As the security guard to Ottawa's Museum of Nature approached the fourth floor walkway, Patrick thought he sensed a subtle change in the man's gait; as though he walked with a slight bit of caution, a feeling of trepidation.
>
> This was always the best part.
>
> The anticipatory adrenaline rush flooded him as he prepared his assault.

There are multiple theories about who might be haunting the building.

One is that the ghost is that of David Ewort, the architect who designed the museum. There are unsupported and unsubstantiated rumors that Ewort killed himself by leaping from the roof, distraught that the building would possibly have to come down due to the tower supposedly separating from the building. That theory, of course, was later disproved.

Some believe that the ghost might be that of a former prime minister. The building, after all, was used as the emergency headquarters for Parliament after the great fire of 1916 destroyed the Parliament Buildings. And Prime Minister Sir Wilfrid Laurier's body lay in state in the museum's auditorium in 1919.

Others believe that whatever haunts the building might be spirits that are attached to the many exhibits that have passed through the museum since it first opened in 1912. "At one point there were mummies in the basement, when it was part of the Museum of Man, which is now the Museum of Civilization," Dan Smythe of media relations for the Museum of Nature said.

During the Halloween season, the museum conducts collaborative tours of the building along with the folks from Haunted Walks. During those tours you'll learn more about the history of the building and hear several of the creepy tales.

But visiting the museum at any time of the year is an excellent educational experience, offering endless possibilities for exploring science and the natural world. And perhaps, if the elements are aligned, a little something from the "super-natural" world.

Conclusion

Ottawa will always be a special city to me, and not just because it the place where I first lived after moving away from the parental homestead, entered university, and got a chance to explore and learn about the world.

And it's not just because the magnificent Haunted Walks tours introduced me to the concept that, despite a lifetime of believing that the past was dull and stagnant, history could come alive with good storytelling and bring the listener or reader right into the moment to properly understand the hearts, minds, and spirits of the people who came before us.

If you cast aside the concept of the spirits and ghastly tales that have been collected in the book and you pause, for just one moment, while standing in the midst of either one of Ottawa's downtown streets, in the heart of the Byward Market or one of the quieter residential suburbs, you may just feel what I feel: the vibrant heartbeat of the place in which the core of our country was formed. And not just through the words and actions of people like the Fathers of Confederation, or those who we trusted enough to vote into power and speak for the people. The heartbeat comes from every man, woman, and child who lived and still lives in this region, the very lifeblood of what makes a community, what makes a place special and unique. What makes a place a home.

The culture and flavour of Ottawa is so fascinating to me. Having grown up in a small mid-northern–Ontario town, where a place like

Sudbury is considered a big city, and having spent so many years working in the heart of Canada's largest city, Toronto, just like Goldilocks I have found Ottawa to be a city that is "just right."

It's not so big that there isn't a strong sense of community and neighbourly spirit, and it's not so small that there isn't a bustling and lively music, arts, and entertainment scene with hundreds of great choices for any particular afternoon or evening.

I haven't lived in Ottawa since 1997, but my heart shall forever remain there, haunting the streets and buildings where I used to roam.

Ghost Walks and
Great Resources

Part of the joy of researching and writing this book has been the amazing reading I was able to do, as well as the things I was able to experience in person. The tours offered by Haunted Walk of Ottawa were the very first historic ghost walks I had the pleasure of taking (and were perhaps the genesis of my love of listening to, collecting, and sharing historic ghost tales). Ottawa on its own is a city so rich in culture and history that just taking an afternoon stroll in the downtown and Byward Market areas is an adventure in learning — not just about the city, its history, and people, but about our country as well.

Below are some of the places and resources that I found myself returning to again and again as I was putting this book together.

The Haunted Walk of Ottawa
46 ½ Sparks Street, Ottawa, ON K1P 5A8
(613) 232-0344
www.hauntedwalk.com/ottawa-tours

Since 1996, Haunted Walk tour guides have been entertaining and educating local residents and tourists with intriguing tales of Ottawa's dark past, involving mysterious murders, ghosts, and hauntings. The founder and director of Haunted Walk, Glen Shackleton, wrote *Ghosts of Ottawa: From the Files of the Haunted Walk*, which is a great walking-tour keepsake.

Bytown Museum
1 Canal Lane, Ottawa
(613) 234-4570
www.bytownmuseum.com

Opened in 1917 by the Women's Canadian Historical Society of Ottawa, the Bytown Museum explores Ottawa's (formerly Bytown's) history and the stories of its residents. Located on the lower locks of the Rideau Canal between Parliament Hill and the Château Laurier hotel, the museum is housed inside the Commissariat, Ottawa's oldest — and most haunted — stone building.

The Toronto and Ontario Ghosts and Hauntings Research Society
www.torontoghosts.org

Numerous tales of paranormal events and experiences are documented here by the Toronto and Ontario Ghosts and Hauntings Research Society, a web-based not-for-profit group dedicated to collecting and investigating reports of ghosts and hauntings from around Ontario. They are the oldest established website of their kind in Canada and are affiliated with Paranormal Studies and Inquiry Canada (PSICAN).

Creepy Canada
http://web.archive.org/web/20080106163700/http://www.creepy.tv/

Aired between 2002 and 2006, *Creepy Canada* is a television series, hosted and produced by Terry Boyle, focusing on Canadian ghost stories and other paranormal activities. It also aired on Destination America in

2014, under the alternate title *Hauntings and Horrors*. Many of the episodes are still available to watch on YouTube.

SELECTED READINGS

Colombo, John Robert. *The Big Book of Canadian Ghost Stories*. Toronto: Dundurn, 2008.

———. *Ghost Stories of Ontario*. Toronto: Dundurn, 1995.

———. *Jeepers Creepers: Canadian Accounts of Weird Events and Experiences*. Toronto: Dundurn, 2011.

———. *The Midnight Hour: Canadian Accounts of Eerie Experiences*. Toronto: Dundurn, 2004.

———. *Mysteries of Ontario*. Toronto: Dundurn, 1999.

———. *Strange But True: Canadian Stories of Horror and Terror*. Toronto: Dundurn, 2005.

Leslie, Mark. *Haunted Hamilton: The Ghosts of Dundurn Castle and Other Steeltown Shivers*. Toronto: Dundurn, 2012.

———. *Tomes of Terror: Haunted Bookstores and Libraries*. Toronto: Dundurn, 2014.

Leslie, Mark, and Jenny Jelen. *Spooky Sudbury: True Tales of the Eerie & Unexplained*. Toronto: Dundurn, 2013.

Scott, Clifford R. *Ottawa Stories: Trials and Triumphs in Bytown History*. Toronto: Dundurn, 2014.

Sources

BOOKS

Boyle, Terry. *Haunted: Ghostly Inns, Hotels, and Other Eerie Places*, 2nd Edition. Toronto: Dundurn, 2013.

Chamney, R. Pearl, and Myrtle H. Adams. "The Ghost of the Normal School." *1916–17 Year Book of the Ottawa Normal School*. Ottawa: Ottawa Normal School, 1917.

Colombo, John Robert. *Ghost Stories of Canada*. Toronto: Dundurn, 2000.

_____. *Ghost Stories of Ontario*. Toronto: Dundurn, 1995.

_____. *The Midnight Hour: Canadian Accounts of Eerie Experiences*. Toronto: Dundurn, 2004.

_____. *Mysteries of Ontario*. Toronto: Dundurn, 1999.

Cook, Sharon Anne. *Sex, Lies, and Cigarettes: Canadian Women, Smoking, and Visual Culture*. Montreal: McGill-Queen's University Press, 2012.

Leslie, Mark. "Hereinafter Referred to as the Ghost." *Tesseracts Seventeen*. Edmonton: Edge Publishing, 2013.

_____. *Tomes of Terror: Haunted Bookstores and Libraries*. Toronto: Dundurn, 2014.

Rutkowski, Chris A. *The Big Book of UFOs*. Toronto: Dundurn, 2010.

_____, and Geoff Dittman. *The Canadian UFO Report: The Best Cases Revealed*. Toronto: Dundurn, 2006.

Scott, Cliff Robinson. *Trials and Triumphs in Bytown History*. Toronto: The History Press, 2014.

Shackleton, Glen. *Ghosts of Ottawa*. Vancouver: Trafford Publishing, 2008.

Stacey, C.P. *A Very Double Life: The Private World of Mackenzie King*. Toronto: Macmillan of Canada, 1996.

Sutherland, Joel A. *Haunted Canada 4: More True Tales of Terror*. Toronto: Scholastic Canada Ltd., 2014.

Telfer, Geordie. *Mysterious Ontario: Myths, Murders, Mysteries and Legends*. Edmonton: Quagmire Press Ltd., 2012.

Wells, Allen R. *The First Canadian: William Lyon Mackenzie King 1874–1950*. New York: Xlibris, 2014.

NEWSPAPERS

"A Little Too Previous." *Quebec Saturday Budget*. December 3, 1892.

"American Television Networks Investigate Unexplained UFO Sightings Near Almonte." *Almonte Gazette*. February 3, 1993.

"Anecdote of Sir John Thompson." *Daily Mail and Empire*. December 4, 1897.

"Attempt Emphasizes Need of New Jail." *Ottawa Citizen*. January 5, 1946.

"Bytown's Haunted House." *Ottawa Citizen*. January 27, 1950.

"Carleton County Jail Plans 'Up in Air' Says Controller." *Ottawa Citizen*. May 17, 1965.

Carmichael, David. "Mackenzie King's Spooky Ruins." *Montreal Gazette*. July 17, 1971.

"Chichester Ghost Was Sensation: Spirit Drowned Man Seen Often." *Ottawa Citizen*. April 19, 1929.

"Clothes Pulled Off Bed By Ghostly Hands on Augusta St." *Ottawa Citizen*. January 31, 1931.

Collard, Edgar Andrew. "All Our Yesterdays: Did D'Arcy McGee Foresee His Sudden Death?" *Montreal Gazette*. November 16, 1963.

Corbett, Ron. "The Story of Muskrat Lake Monster." *Ottawa Sun*. July 27, 2014.

"D'Arcy McGee's Murderer." *The Times*. June 2, 1876.

Dodge, Brier. "Halloween Haunts Planned for Carleton Place." *Almonte Canadian Gazette*. October 20, 2011.

"Earl Wilson, Old Time Stuff Editor, Dies." *Ottawa Citizen*. March 22, 1955.

"The Family Dog Ended Ghost Story." *Ottawa Citizen*. August 6, 1932.

"Ghostly Violin Player Haunted a Stone House Near L'Orignal." *Ottawa Citizen*. March 8, 1930.

"Grand Jury Report: Medieval Jail Needs Action." *Ottawa Citizen*. January 1969.

Hanzidiakou, Molly. "The Haunted History of Ottawa." *Glue*. October 29, 2013.

"In Carleton County Jail for 31 Days." *Ottawa Citizen*. April 24, 1915.

"Insane in Jails." *Ottawa Citizen*. December 9, 1909.

King, Melanie. "Elizabeth Barnes: The Witch of Plum Hollow." *The Country Collection*. Issue 41, Winter 2003.

"Laid the Ghost." *Ottawa Citizen*. July 21, 1923.

Lanktree, Graham. "Hotel's Founder May Be Link to Château Laurier's 100-Year-Old Haunting." *Metro Ottawa*. October 31, 2012.

Majerczyk, Julius. "Rescuing History: Old Mill Will Return to Working Order." *Ottawa Citizen*. September 22, 1975.

MUFON Ontario. "Uncovering the Guardian Caper." *MUFON UFO Journal*. May 1994.

"My Ghostly Guide." *Ottawa Free Press*. January 15, 1891.

"Mystery of a Missing Moose Solved By Old Mother Barnes." *Ottawa Citizen*. February 8, 1936.

Neal, Christopher. "Mill Offers Grist for Believers in Ghosts." *Ottawa Citizen*. Tuesday, July 29, 1986.

Nolan, Dermot P. "Thomas D'Arcy McGee: A Canadian Martyr." *Hamilton Spectator*. April 8, 2015.

"Old Dr. Van Cortlandt House and its Ghostly Stories." *Ottawa Citizen*. April 29, 1933.

"Ottawa Tours Get Into Spirit of Capital's Ghostly Past." *Waterloo Region Record*. January 28, 2011.

"People Were Puzzled About Haunted House." *Ottawa Citizen*. January 19, 1935.

"Plum Hollow Witch Still Casts Spell." *Ottawa Citizen*. October 28, 1982.

"Recalled Uncanny Prediction When Close to Death's Door." *Ottawa Citizen*. February 8, 1935.

Robin, Laura. "New Beckta Dininy & Wine to Open on Elgin St., Nov 19." *Ottawa Citizen*. September 17, 2014.

"Sailors Claim Boat Was Haunted." *Ottawa Citizen*. October 1, 1926.

Skuce, Marsh. "City Has No Interest in Elgin Street Property." *Ottawa Citizen*. October 1, 1974.

Steiner, Lorie Lee. "Towers of Time: The Thomas Fuller Legacy." *Country Connection Magazine*. Issue 52, Summer 2006.

"Story of the Mystifying Noise in a Farm House: Ghost that Sighed or Gasped and Moved About." *Ottawa Citizen*. March 8, 1930.

"Urges Moving of Carleton County Jail to Country." *Ottawa Citizen*. October 3, 1945.

"Was it Ghost of a Dead Youth that Cummings Children Saw." *Ottawa Citizen*. July 16, 1932.

"Weird Light in Old Cunningham Hotel Nearly Scared Farmer's Wife to Death." *Ottawa Citizen*. March 29, 1929.

VIDEOS

Brown, Patrick, and Wilder Tweedale. "The Ghosts of Watson's Mill." www.youtube.com/watch?v=ajn4ZHCY95A.

"Carleton Place, Paranormal Investigation Heritage Inn Redo." CHAPS Paranormal. www.youtube.com/watch?v=W4SfkUex0Vs.

Creepy Canada. "Ghost of Ann Crosby," Episode 1. Produced by Brian O'Dea, OLN. October 23, 2002.

Lamb, Melissa. "My Haunted Ottawa — Museum of Nature." *CTV Ottawa Morning Live*. www.youtube.com/watch?v=KljwV0DGuUw. October 26, 2011.

"'Lone Woman' Photo Investigation." The Haunted Walk. hauntedwalk.com/videos.

"My Haunted Ottawa: Watson's Mill." *CTV Morning Live*. www.youtube.com/watch?v=n0-yRz0Vn3s. October 28, 2011.

WEBSITES

"24 Sussex Drive." National Capital Commission. www.ncc-ccn.gc.ca/places-to-visit/official-residences/24-sussex-drive.

"About the Mackenzie King Estate." National Capital Commission. www.ncc-ccn.gc.ca/places-to-visit/mackenzie-king-estate/about-mackenzie-king-estate.

"The Arnprior & District Museum." The Toronto and Ontario Ghosts and Hauntings Research Society. www.torontoghosts.org/index.php?/20120621742/Eastern-Ontario/The-Arnprior-District-Museum.html.

"Billings, Bradish, Jr." Biographical Dictionary of Architects in Canada 1800–1950. www.dictionaryofarchitectsincanada.org/node/1118.

"Carleton County Gaol." Canada's Historic Places. www.historicplaces.ca/en/rep-reg/place-lieu.aspx?id=8443.

"Carp — Richardson Side Road." The Toronto and Ontario Ghosts and Hauntings Research Society. www.torontoghosts.org/index.php?/20090513624/Eastern-Ontario/Carp-Richardson-Side-Road.html.

"The Carp Case: The MUFON Ontario Version." The Virtually Strange Network. www.virtuallystrange.net/ufo/mufonontario/archive/carp.html.

"The Carp/Guardian Case." Canadian X-Files. ufo-joe.tripod.com/cases/1989carp.html#lightfoot.

DeCoste, Erin. "Ottawa Hostel in the Top 10 of World's Spookiest Buildings." *CTV News*, October 31, 2011. www.ctvnews.ca/ottawa-hostel-in-top-10-of-world-s-spookiest-buildings-1.719205.

Devoy, Desmond. "Guido's is Getting Ready to Party this Summer." Inside Ottawa Valley, March 11, 2011. www.insideottawavalley.com/news-story/3801055-guido-s-is-getting-ready-to-party-this-summer.

"Diaries of William Lyon Mackenzie King." Library and Archives Canada. www.bac-lac.gc.ca/eng/discover/politics-government/prime-ministers/william-lyon-mackenzie-king/Pages/diaries-william-lyon-mackenzie-king.aspx.

Dillabough, Lyle. "The Tale of Stompin' Tom Connors Riding Into Town." Heritage Carleton Place. www.heritagecarletonplace.com/3/miscellaneous3.htm.

Ellis, Larry. "The Good Life." Watson's Mill. www.watsonsmill.com/Community.html.

Foran, Lindsay. "Top 5 Most Haunted Places in Ottawa." yp nexthome. http://nexthome.yp.ca/news/top-5-most-haunted-places-in-ottawa/15379/.

"Grant House Freshens Up." Images of Centretown, November 10, 2010. http://centretown.blogspot.ca/2010/11/grant-house-freshens-up.html.

Grenier, Danika. "Bumping up Beckta's fine dining experience at 150 Elgin." Ottawa Tourism, January 9, 2015. www.ottawatourism.ca/ottawa-insider/bumping-up-becktas-fine-dining-experience-at-150-elgin.

Hall, Ashley. "Faceless Ghosts." The Paranormal Guide, April 24, 2013. www.theparanormalguide.com/blog/faceless-ghosts.

"Haunted Arnprior, Part II." Aerendel. www.aerendel.ca/haunted/Haunted02.html.

Hempstead, Doug. "Stompin' Tom Connors credited with saving Carleton Place hotel." Ottawa Sun, March 7, 2013. www.ottawasun.com/2013/03/07/stompin-tom-connors-credited-with-saving-carleton-place-hotel.

"Heritage Buildings." Heritage Carleton Place. www.heritagecarleton-place.com/3/miscellaneous1.htm.

"Heritage Inn: Carleton Place, Ontario." CHAPS Paranormal. www.chapsparanormal.ca/chaps/investigations/2009-01_CarletonPlace.html.

"HI-Ottawa Jail." Hostelling International Canada. www.hihostels.ca/Ontario/1166/HI-Ottawa-Jail.hostel.

"History." Courtyard Restaurant. www.courtyardrestaurant.com/history/.

"History and Buildings." Canadian Museum of Nature. http://nature.ca/en/about-us/history-buildings.

Kulp, Ashley. "Couple Gives Historic Carleton Place Hotel New Lease on Life." Inside Ottawa Valley (July 31, 2014). www.insideotta-wavalley.com/news-story/4729173-couple-gives-historic-carleton-place-hotel-new-lease-on-life/.

PSICAN International. "Paranormal Studies and Investigations Canada: General Information & Codes of Governance/Presentation." PSICAN International, January 28, 2012. www.psican.org/PSICAN_Gen-Inf_Codes.pdf.

Schiering-Toll, Tiffany. "The Canadian museum of nature: one of Ottawa's most notorious haunts." *The Examiner*, March 30, 2012. www.examiner.com/article/the-canadian-museum-of-nature-one-of-ottawa-s-most-notorious-haunts.

Seccaspina, Linda. "Architecture Stories — The Grand Ole Lady of Carleton Place, Ontario." Zoomer. http://connect.everythingzoomer.com/profiles/blogs/architecture-stories-the-grand-ole-lady-of-carleton-place-ontario.

_____. "Walking with Ghosts — The Hauntings of Ida Moore." Zoomer, September 15, 2013. http://connect.everythingzoomer.com/profiles/blogs/walking-with-ghosts-the-ghost-of-ida-moore.

Slawych, Diane. "Sprit lingers at Canada's historic hotels." 24Hrs Vancouver. http://vancouver.24hrs.ca/Lifestyle/travel/2010/10/25/15822656.html.

"Watson's Mill History." Watson's Mill. www.watsonsmill.com/Mill_History.html.

Willing, Jon. "Did UFO Crash into Ottawa River?" Welland Tribune, July 28, 2009. www.wellandtribune.ca/2009/07/28/did-ufo-crash-into-ottawa-river.

By the Same Author

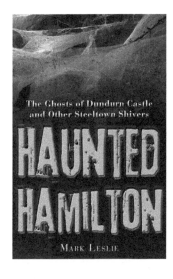

Haunted Hamilton
Mark Leslie

From the Hermitage ruins to Dundurn Castle, from the Customs House to Stoney Creek Battlefield Park, the city of Hamilton, Ontario, is steeped in a rich history and culture. But beneath the surface of the Steel City there dwells a darker heart — from the shadows of yesteryear arise the unexplainable, the bizarre, and the chilling.

Lock the doors and turn on all the lights before you settle down with this book, because once you begin to read about the supernatural elements that lurk within this seemingly normal city in Southern Ontario, strange bumps in the night will take on new, more sinister meanings. Prepare to be thrilled and chilled with this collection of tales compiled from historical documents, first-person accounts, and the files of the paranormal group Haunted Hamilton, which has been investigating and celebrating Hamilton's historic haunted past since 1999.

Tomes of Terror
Mark Leslie

Throughout history, books have inspired, informed, entertained, and enriched us. They have also kept us up through the night, thrilled us, and lured us into their endless depths. *Tomes of Terror* is a celebration and an eerie look at the siren call of literature and the unexplained and fascinating stories associated with bookish locations around the world.

Mark Leslie's latest paranormal page-turner is a compendium of true stories of the supernatural in literary locales, complete with hair-raising first-person accounts. You may even recognize a spectre of your local library lurking in these true stories and photographs. If you have ever felt an indescribable presence hanging about a quiet bookshop, then you'll enjoy these fascinating and haunting tales.

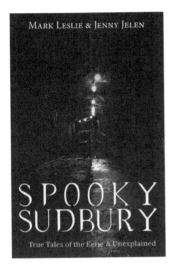

Spooky Sudbury
Mark Leslie and Jenny Jelen

"I tried to leave" is a common refrain for those from the Sudbury region. People often vow to move away, but something about the Nickel City keeps luring them back. Whether it's the taste of fresh air — or just the sulphur in the air — it's hard to move beyond the black rocks, endless lakes, and great openness without longing to come home.

Some are so attached to the northern community that they choose to stick around, even when their physical life is over. After all, if the living can't leave the place behind, why should the dead?

Spooky Sudbury explores the magnetic aura surrounding the city, for the living as well as the once-alive, in these tales of the supernatural.

Available at your favourite bookseller